Londoners Making London

LUND
HUMPHRIES

Londoners Making London

Transforming Neighbourhoods Jan Kattein

First published in 2024 by Lund Humphries
Lund Humphries
Huckletree Shoreditch
Alphabeta Building
18 Finsbury Square
London EC2A 1AH
UK

www.lundhumphries.com

Londoners Making London: Transforming Neighbourhoods
© Jan Kattein, 2024

All rights reserved

ISBN: 978-1-84822-452-0

A Cataloguing-in-Publication record for this book is available from the British Library

All rights reserved. No part of this publication may be reproduced, stored in a retrieval system or transmitted in any form or by any means, electrical, mechanical or otherwise, without first seeking the permission of the copyright owners and publishers. Every effort has been made to seek permission to reproduce the images in this book. Any omissions are entirely unintentional, and details should be addressed to the publishers.

Jan Kattein has asserted his right under the Copyright, Designs and Patent Act, 1988, to be identified as the Author of this Work.

Copy edited by Karen Francis
Designed by Gareth Marriott
Cover design by Myfanwy Vernon-Hunt, This Side
Set in Graphik and Circular Std
Printed in Bosnia and Hezegovina
Front cover image: Blue House Yard, Jan Kattein Architects

This book is printed on sustainably sourced FSC paper

Contents

Acknowledgements	9
Introduction	11
Chapter 1: Ecology + Leadership	**17**
The Skip Garden *[with Jane Riddiford]*	20
Sitopia Farm *[with Chloë Dunnett]*	48
Chapter 2: Enterprise + Learning	**69**
Thornhill Library *[with Kate Slotover + Emily Bohill]*	72
The Tailoring Academy *[with Jenny Holloway]*	94
Church Grove *[with Anurag Verma + Jon Broome]*	112
Chapter 3: Building + Making	**127**
Blue House Yard *[with Alice Hardy]*	130
Maxilla Men's Shed *[with Rasha El-Sady]*	152
Chapter 4: Temporality + Activation	**167**
African Street Style *[with Jeffrey Lennon]*	170
Food Bus *[with Kemi Akinola]*	188
Creativity, Authorship + Governance	**204**
About the Author	*208*
Bibliography	*209*
Image Credits	*210*
Index	*212*

'You never change things by fighting the existing reality. To change something, build a new model that makes the existing model obsolete.'

Richard Buckminster Fuller

Acknowledgements

This book has been five years in the making. Throughout that period many people have contributed their time and their ideas, formally and informally. Early versions were conceived with Jack Sallabank, whose contribution was instrumental in formulating the proposal and building momentum. Kirsty McMullan did valuable research to identify contributors. The team at Jan Kattein Architects and in particular Felicity Barbur, Robert Baron, Heloise Desaissement, Gareth Marriott, Chandni Patel, Corina Tuna and Gabriel Warshafsky have implemented several of the projects that are featured and have, during many discussions in the studio, contributed to shaping the intellectual narrative that supports our work.

Thank you to the many clients and partners who have been trusting when embarking on sometimes quite unconventional ways of delivering their projects, in particular Pippa Gueterbock, Beth Kay and Eric Osei at Haringey Council, Andrew Forsey at Feeding Britain, Emily Berwyn and Eddie Bridgeman at Meanwhile Space, the students of Unit 3 at The Bartlett who designed and made the Skip Garden, and the whole team at Global Generation.

Thank you to The Bartlett School of Architecture for funding the research that has gone into the book and to my editor Valerie Rose at Lund Humphries who has had infinite patience and has always given words of encouragement and reassurance.

Thank you to my wife Chrysanthe Staikopoulou, without whose intellectual contribution the book would not have been what it is. Thank you to the photographers who have taken the images in the book. And lastly thank you to Kemi Akinola, Emily Bohill, Jon Broome, Chloë Dunnett, Rasha El-Sady, Alice Hardy, Jenny Holloway, Jeffrey Lennon, Jane Riddiford, Kate Slotover and Anurag Verma who all have, despite their busy lives, been generous in giving their time and sharing their ideas.

To Melina, Nefeli and Emilia, who are finding their own ways of shaping their world as they grow up.

Introduction

This book tells the story of nine projects that have redefined neighbourhoods through the eyes of those involved. Interviews with instigators, community activists, campaigners and self-builders illuminate the projects from an experiential and personal angle. The book talks about London and about Londoners.

City-making is often seen as the domain of professionals, architects, planners and engineers. Yet, transformational change is increasingly driven by people. Communities coming together to change their neighbourhoods for the better. Young and old working as one to create places that better meet their needs, that support well-being and give people a sense of belonging. Those formerly excluded from town planning are starting to tackle deficiencies from the bottom up.

Areas such as Wandsworth, Shoreditch and Wood Green can all tell incredibly important stories of change which has brought people together. Be it street parties, urban gardening, invigorated empty spaces or redesigned neighbourhoods, they all have a story to tell that illustrates what can be done when people work together.

I met my interviewees through my work with municipalities, NGOs and communities in London. Some of the projects that I have included, my colleagues at Jan Kattein Architects have implemented. However, the book is not about architects or architecture; it is about those individuals who, through their passion, conviction and determination, and often against all odds, created better places for and with their communities.

The methodology that I have used in writing this book is a close reflection of how we practise at Jan Kattein Architects. Design for us is never the result of singular authorship and is instead shaped by a diversity of voices. That is true also for this book. My role when practising and when writing is to instigate the conversation and then to identify and name prevailing and contrasting concerns, views and observations and to build common ground.

What really interested me when I set out to write *Londoners Making London* was whether there are parallels, recurring themes, methods or approaches that connect the projects and their initiators, and what we might learn from them. And whilst every project and the experience of its authors is highly individual, it is only when people come together and share their insight that we can scale our impact. I have grouped the case studies into four chapters in accordance with the principal themes that define the projects: Ecology + Leadership; Learning + Enterprise; Building + Making; and Temporality + Activation.

With the selection of the nine projects that I have included, I do not want to make a quality judgement. There are hundreds if not thousands of other examples out there that are equally laudable and impactful and that deserve to have their story told. The selection is initially the result of pragmatism.

Projects where I had contacts and access to photographs made it onto the shortlist. Those that volunteered to contribute were interviewed. There was, however, an unexpected benefit which has validated the approach that I took. Working with partners who had sometimes become friends meant that a space of trust was created during the interviews where interviewees felt comfortable to convey personal insights or experiences that have been instrumental in crystallising their motivation. As with many of the stories in the book, the book itself has been a way to mobilise people to contribute, to share their expertise and to inspire others.

The title of the book is deliberate. It talks about people, making as a creative and productive activity, and a unique place, London.

LONDONERS

What is it that makes a Londoner a Londoner? Statistically London is the most multicultural city in Europe. More than 30 per cent of its inhabitants were born in another country. It is also a transient city. Many of those driving change have come from elsewhere. Many of the contributors to this book (myself included) are first- or second-generation immigrants or have moved to London from other parts of the UK. As a commuter city, London's population swells by more than 12 per cent during the working day, shrinking by the same at night.

This book defines a Londoner by their contribution to civic society, by their commitment to public life and by their concern for the well-being of others. The book suggests that, in London, belonging and affiliation are perhaps more readily defined by personal investment than by origin or place of birth. London has a unique capacity to co-opt all those prepared to help advance its perpetual social and spatial remaking, irrespective of where they come from.

The stories that are told in this book demonstrate their protagonists' unrelenting enthusiasm for making London better for its citizens. In their own way, each one of them has found their niche and their voice, often outside the norm and in the absence of funding. Yet, contributors are neither activists nor conformists. Through stealth or serendipity they manage to circumnavigate process and procedure. They employ their creativity to identify and prise open gaps in the system to cultivate critical dialogue and togetherness.

In fact, one might argue that their greatest success is their ability to challenge the way things are usually done. Where Jeffrey Lennon's African Street Style Festival disrupts the customary use of the street by replacing cars with people, Chloë Dunnett's organic farm produces commercial quantities of organic food, yet her practice also constitutes an act of protest against an unjust and unsustainable food system.

As a creative practitioner, I know that pessimism and creativity are diametric concepts. Creativity needs the space and assuredness that only optimism yields. The practices of the people who have contributed to this book are shaped by this duality, a questioning of the status quo by demonstrating what a more just and equitable alternative would look like. Their job is twice as hard, as they must accomplish two tasks: to verbalise the deficiency that they lament as well as providing a grounded vision of how to fix it.

Rasha El-Sady's advice in her story about Maxilla Men's Shed is to the point: '… I would say challenge the way it's done and look at more creative ways of getting those outcomes.'

What is unique about London and about Londoners is people's preparedness to value personal investment and engagement over conformity and adaptation. Where the objectives are equitable, just and inclusive, a Londoner, maybe ahead of any other metropolitan citizen, will embrace the mantra that the end justifies the means.

MAKING

A maker employs their creativity and industry to produce goods or to forward social change. A place-maker embraces spatial practice for the same ends. The term 'making' in the title of this book can best be understood in this context. Change-makers are often those that effect policy and practice through spatial transformation.

To make is to have purpose. Yet, making – as opposed to fabrication – suggests an iterative approach that is more closely associated with craft than with manufacturing. Sociologist Richard Sennett observes that craft in the English language is not exclusively associated with manual labour and that it can also be used in the context of other artistic pursuits, such as making music. A craftsperson, Sennett writes, distinguishes themselves through 'their dedication to good work for its own sake'. Crafting, he suggests, 'represents the special human condition of being engaged'. Much the same is true for making. Making, however, is perhaps more communal than crafting. It is also a more inclusive pursuit, as a maker is not necessarily a professional or a specialist in their field. Makers can learn on the job and innovate to solve problems. Makers are inherently creative. Ignorance of professional norms and societal constraints can be an asset, rather than a deficiency. Through curiosity and determination, a maker engages themselves and others. In doing so, they have the capacity to challenge and advance society. It is in this context that I would like to see the term maker in the title of this book understood.

'Making London' references the spatial evolution of the city, but it also refers to the advancement of governance structures and well-being objectives, the creation of opportunities and better community cohesion. My colleague and friend Gabriel Warshafsky wrote, 'We believe that an integrated approach is needed for any place to fulfil its potential'. The term 'making' captures this integration, this advancement irrespective of disciplinary boundaries.

LONDON

London is a city of villages. With nearly 600 high streets and town centres, everyone living and working here associates with their neighbourhood. This structure is particularly effective in preserving London's heterogeneity and empowering communities to effect change locally.

The way that London is governed replicates its polycentric pattern. From geographically smallest to largest entity, there are electoral wards represented by a Councillor who is a member of one of 32 Borough Councils. The overarching regional government is the Greater London Authority, administrated by a directly elected Council and the Mayor of London. Due to the overlap of jurisdiction – the Mayor, for instance, is responsible for the major road network connecting the city strategically, whilst local authorities are responsible for public spaces, parks and services – collaboration and negotiation between stakeholders is intrinsic to the way change is implemented.

Since its inauguration in 2006, the Greater London Authority has been instrumental in promoting a more inclusive, grass-roots form of urbanism. Several of the projects in this book would not have happened without its support. Through research, advocacy, tactical support and campaigning, the Greater London Authority has managed to mobilise local actors to implement change, drawing on the wisdom and networks of those intimately familiar with their locality. Its role is fairly unique and a distinct departure from more traditional, hierarchical local governance styles in Europe.

The programme has led to the creation of thousands of public spaces and community assets, has improved the existing urban environment through direct investment and has established institutions and governance structures to secure the legacy of the places that have been created. By default, the Greater London Authority's approach has built the capacity of thousands of Londoners to autonomously promote and implement change at a neighbourhood level. The tools for placemaking and urban stewardship have effectively been laid at the feet of Londoners.

The collaborative approach propagated in London during the past 17 years has permeated local organisations and authorities and is now informing private-sector methodology. Global Generation's Skip Garden, which is featured in this book, is an example of a community initiative that has for decades benefited from the stewardship of a real estate development company who has provided land and funding and augmented the reach of the charity by co-opting its own network of partners and suppliers to Global Generation's cause. The Skip Garden, which started off as a temporary and movable community food-growing project, became an integral part of the new King's Cross neighbourhood, so much so that the developer recently assigned a permanent site in their legacy development to the project. That land is shortly to be transformed into an educational ecology garden to be operated and maintained in perpetuity by the charity.

London and Londoners have been getting on quietly with the city's transformation. Success is barely recorded and hardly broadcast, a victim of limited resources and a struggle to measure, position and articulate achievements. This book gives those that have initiated or implemented grass-roots projects the opportunity to reflect and to review.

PLANNING

In 1961, Jane Jacobs's seminal work *The Death and Life of Great American Cities* made the case for citizen-led planning processes. Despite a recent resurgence of her work in professional discourse and genuine attempts from designers to reassess their methods, town planning remains as inaccessible to communities as it has ever been. The Department for Digital, Culture, Media and Sport Community Life Survey from 2020/21 finds that only 27 per cent of people in the UK feel that they can influence decisions that affect their local area, despite 54 per cent of people feeling that it is important to be able to do so.

Work undertaken by the Quality of Life Foundation on behalf of the Harlow and Gilston Garden Town makes direct linkages between quality of life and the level of control that local people feel they have over their environment. The Foundation highlights that, in Harlow and Gilston, a sense of disenfranchisement in relation to decisions made about the local area is particularly acute amongst young people.

Specialist tools and inaccessible language continue to relegate town planning to professionals who can read and draw masterplans, have access to data and are literate in digital visualisation. Planners who genuinely have the well-being of communities at heart continue to feel misunderstood, whereas communities often feel that the local wisdom and intelligence that they bring to the table is in the end eclipsed by the power of strategic objectives expressed in obscure jargon, authoritative drawings and irrefutable statistics.

Planning as a way of organising cities is often perceived as slow, academic and ultimately irrelevant to the way people experience their neighbourhoods. The positions may well be irreconcilable, simply because the two factions are looking at the city from two radically different viewpoints. Whereas planning organises spaces from above, communities tend to scrutinise their environment at eye level. The best urbanism comes from merging these two viewpoints. A good city works at a strategic level as well as experientially. Accepting that neither of the two vantage points is wrong and giving greater respect to each other's positions will allow us to build the common ground that we so urgently need to move forward.

LANGUAGE + EQUALITY

Language has an important role to play in maintaining the status quo and is the greatest cause of misunderstanding. Jeffrey Lennon's battle to close a street for a day to host the African Street Style Festival provides a lived illustration of this conundrum. In London, streets make up around 80 per cent of all public space. Yet only 30 per cent of adults in London own a car. The remaining 70 per cent and everyone under 18 has to contend with a legal and perceptual distortion that prevents the reappropriation of public space to better cater for the needs of the majority.

Jurisdiction over streets is vested in the local authority's highways department and in Transport for London, the Mayor's equivalent agency on a regional level. The choice of terminology in the names of these agencies, 'highways' and 'transport', indicates a bias in favour of propulsive movement over play, rest, entertainment and socialising. A simple renaming to, say, 'Department of Public Space' or 'Public Space for London' would immediately suggest a more inclusive remit, promoting a shift of focus towards support for mental and physical well-being.

Daniel Casas-Valle, initiator of the knowledge platform 'the Future Design of Streets', recently said that 'we speak about the right to the city – we need to start speaking about the right to the street'. His statement is a timely reminder of the huge task we face to address the inequalities that the current linguistic and legal framework promotes.

A recent report from the Mayor of London shows communities affected by higher levels of deprivation, and those containing a higher proportion of people from a non-white ethnic background, are more likely to be exposed to higher levels of air pollution. Tackling the challenges presented by climate change and adapting our cities to increase resilience will first and foremost require collaboration. The United Nations Sustainable Development Goal no. 17 advocates exactly this: 'partnership for the goals'. In cities where every square metre of space must answer to multiple, often conflicting priorities, nothing much can be achieved without collaboration and mutual recognition of objectives.

Books about community-led initiatives in cities are often written by and for professionals and academics. I have selected the interview format to give direct and personal insight into processes and projects. But the format also represents an attempt to re-evaluate and evolve the language that we use when we speak about the city. Widening participation in planning and urbanism and reversing the disenfranchisement that young people in particular experience in relation to their physical environment requires us first and foremost to learn to speak and write in a way that is understood by everyone. The interview format gives those who have initiated and implemented change an opportunity to recast professional jargon in their own image.

1/
Ecology
+ Leadership

Londoners Making London

The King's Cross Skip Garden and Sitopia Farm in Greenwich have one important communality. Both projects introduce nature into the city and increase biodiversity locally. Yet, the real success is the shift in the narrative around climate change and biodiversity loss that the projects promote. Their ability to link conservation objectives to issues of inclusivity and social justice gives them great urgency and helps to rally new audiences to their cause. Whilst this link is being made in intellectual discourse elsewhere, including by developing countries affected by climate change, a practice that arises from it here in London is rare.

For both projects, engaging and inspiring a new generation of activists and equipping them with the language and leadership skills to question existing systems and promote environmental justice is critical. Two methods are at the heart of this approach.

Jane Riddiford describes how achieving a shift away from a binary world view of 'us and them' is central to her practice. Focusing on communalities rather than differences builds the community needed to achieve profound change. The aim is to reduce inequality by achieving a change from within that touches both the personal and professional lives of those participating.

Unfettered optimism and a can-do attitude in the face of real-life challenges engages others in Chloë Dunnett's project. Jane often talks about the importance of 'travelling hopeful', a philosophy that advocates for a sense of shared ownership and responsibility for the project and the deficiencies that it seeks to remedy. Chloë speaks in similar terms when she uses the term 'making your luck happen'.

The Skip Garden and Sitopia Farm are 'gardens of a thousand hands', created by many. They embody a critique by creation. They protest against deficiencies by placing the tools to call these deficiencies out and address them in the hands of all those who have become invested in their creation. In doing so, they do not proclaim to represent the one and only solution. They reverse the sense of powerlessness by setting an example, establishing a precedent and canvassing a vision, setting up others to become leaders in the field of ecology.

The proof of concept of Jane's and Chloë's approach can be found in their own biographies. The chance opportunity to rewild a highway cutting in collaboration with a school in Auckland was instrumental in fomenting Jane's motivation. Chloë describes her experience of growing a vegetable patch as a child and then establishing a patchwork farm in London before finally setting up Sitopia Farm.

Kurt Lewin first established the term 'action research' at the Massachusetts Institute of Technology in 1964 as a methodology which sequentially oscillates planning, social action and analysis. The methodology is relevant to many of the projects in this book. Action research benefits the cause through near-immediate social impact whilst simultaneously developing Jane's and Chloë's practice from garden to garden and season to season. Although neither of the two uses quantitative analysis, evaluation is built into the seasonally iterative process. A gardener learns by doing, discovering what species thrive in the sun or in the shade, in loamy or chalky soils. Sitopia Farm achieved financial stability after two years of operation and Global Generation's programmes have multiplied their reach by expanding to three gardens in several locations in London.

The Skip Garden w/ Jane Riddiford

2015 – 2019

London, King's Cross, N1C

About

Dr Jane Riddiford grew up in New Zealand. Her first rewilding project established a learning resource for young people in an urban area in Auckland. When Jane came to the UK, she managed environmental education programmes for young people in London and Wiltshire before she co-founded the charity Global Generation in 2004.

Her dedication to bringing communities together through storytelling and hands-on reflective experiences has defined her practice. In 2016 she was awarded a DProf in Organisational Change from Middlesex University and Ashridge Business School. Through an action research approach, her inquiry drew on experiences within Global Generation and focused on how the living story of ecology and the wider cosmos can support collaborative approaches to leadership within an organisation. Jane is the author of the book *Learning to Lead Together – An Ecological and Community Approach*.

From 2009 to 2019 the Skip Garden in King's Cross was central to Global Generation's activities. The garden moved site four times during these ten years, making space for the ongoing rebuilding of the area. Jan Kattein and Julia King were teaching a design studio at The Bartlett School of Architecture in 2014 and, together with their students, the studio worked with Global Generation to design and build the final iteration of the garden on a site on Tapper Walk.

The project became one of the most visited urban gardens in London, attracting up to 10,000 visitors annually. The Skip Garden is now closed, but Global Generation has set up other gardens: the Story Garden at the British Library, the Floating Garden at Granary Square and the Paper Garden at Canada Water. Jane has returned to New Zealand, where she is working on her second book and setting up an environmental charity to rewild the banks of an ancient river course that had been straightened by agriculture.

1.01 : [previous page] - Detail of Rachael Taylor's Glass House Lantern at the Skip Garden.

Chapter 1 | Ecology + Leadership

JK   JR   JK   JR

Jan: Jane, thank you for meeting. I want to go a little bit back to the time before the Skip Garden. Your story starts far away from London and way before you founded Global Generation. You often speak about the planting of a forest in New Zealand. Can you explain how this experience has laid the foundations of your practice?

Jane: Wow, that's a wonderful question and I don't always get asked that directly. I think the short answer is, it was then that I learned that growing a forest is growing a community. You've probably read my account of the story of it. I was living across a six-lane motorway with a bank that had been stripped bare by the creation of that motorway. And there was a school above it, on the hill. I was studying horticulture at the time with an interest in sustainable land management, and I used to sit and have my breakfast and imagine, gosh, what would that hill be like if it was once again covered in the mantle of the dark green, New Zealand bush.

I would just sit there and imagine that. And it turned out that my next-door neighbour

1.02 : Dr Jane Riddiford, Founding Director of Global Generation.

was the governor of the school. And I mentioned the idea to her and the board of governors. And she said, 'Oh, I will arrange a meeting with the head teacher.' And I went on to meet this chap called Tim Heath, and we started to dream together.

A dreaming space can also be a very practical space. There was a spark of the possible, and one thing led to another. And it was not so long after that, that this idea of an inner-city forest began to form. And we started a plant nursery around the school swimming pool and the children collected seeds and grew things from the seeds. Then we got funding, and I would go in once a week, and then we'd have volunteer days. I remember that some of the children were Pacific Islanders. It was a special occasion to work on the forest. And I remember some of them showing up in white frilly dresses to work on the forest. I knew from that moment that it would be a special place. And we invited local people too, who originally lived on the land. They blessed the land at the start. That felt very significant. It had been a contested area. There were two different tribes. And we planted the forest as you would do in new native forests, which is successional, in layers. We first covered the bank in logs and branches and grew the forest slowly and iteratively. This laid the foundations for how we developed Global Generation's projects, involving everybody and away from the ground upwards and slowly and iteratively.

And we added other creative inquiry into the practical business of planting trees, such as drawing, writing and storytelling. Then I came to live in England. It was quite a few years later that I went to see the forest. The climax species were poking through, and

23

Londoners Making London

1.03 : Children watering.

Chapter 1 | Ecology + Leadership

JK   JR

the native birds were there and the school had started a food-growing programme. I was so struck, I felt so privileged to have walked hand in hand and participated in the processes of nature. Creating a forest is like creating a nursery of plants and also a nursery of ideas and a nursery of possibility.

Jan: Then you came to London – a radically different environment, or maybe not? What was your way in?

Jane: When I first came to London, I volunteered at Camley Street Natural Park; and that's when I first got to know King's Cross. And then I got a job with an organisation called Camden Jobtrain. I worked with young people who'd been expelled from school. We developed a project called Fitzroy Park opposite the ladies' bathing pond in Hampstead. I was into organic gardening, and I worked with someone who was head gardener at Kenwood House. She thought that I was a real cowboy. She was busy mowing the lawns perfectly and giving them sharp edges. And I was growing food. Quite the opposite. This was around 2000. There was the civil war in the Balkans. Friends of mine who were working in theatre were going down. They had these large puppets, a big friendly giant, and an old Post Office van. They went to the camps in Macedonia and worked with refugees. Anyway, I got involved with them when they returned to London, and we worked with refugees here. The organisation was called Rise Phoenix. We were increasingly working with young people in Camden. One of the trustees had this land in Wiltshire on an organic farm called Pertwood. We took some of the children to Pertwood. We brought four very different groups, young people from

1.04 : Looking after the planted skips.
1.05 : Interior of the Glass House Lantern

25

1.06 : Iman Mohd Hadzhalie's prototype Vertical Living Landscape made from used glass bottles.

Chapter 1 | Ecology + Leadership

JK JR

the housing estates in Kentish Town, some pupils from a country school and young people from a private school. There were about 50 of them with us in Pertwood. We had this wonderful experience of them all connecting with the land and somehow the difference between them dropped. And I thought there is something in this, there are a lot of commonalities. I remember my mother coming and volunteering. She was probably in her eighties at the time, she'd come over from New Zealand. Some of the other people who were involved with us were from Jamaica, and my mum had this feeling of it melting away her own racism, as she put it. And I thought, this is about connecting to nature, but it is also about providing opportunities for people to connect to each other who wouldn't normally meet, and about creating an environment where that was possible. So that's why we have this rather big name, Global Generation. The meaning of Global is about a perspective that's beyond differences and creating opportunities to live our way into that, I think.

Jan: Would you call what you do activism? I sense that an element of challenge of how things are done and how they are perceived is integral to your work. And there is an almost wilful ignorance of convention in your practice.

Jane: I like the way you put that, Jan. I think it's a more benign form of activism, maybe gentle activism. I really cannot bear fundamentalism, of whatever creed. And obviously we have had a lot of it in recent years. I always find it fascinating that people on either end of the spectrum of fundamentalism are often in a very similar place. A lot of my work is about

JK JR

going beyond the binary and occupying that middle place. A lot of people who are involved in the so-called environmental space wouldn't work with developers. As you know from the time when you worked with us, we met great individuals. Maybe the activism is to bring out humanity in all the different ways; whether it's the gardening or the building or just sitting in a circle around the fire, letting people step out of their suits, the entrenchment of their ideas, and to actually just connect and be human beings together. Every time that happens it is so heartening. It is like, oh, right, this is why we are doing what we are doing.

Jan: That's unusual. Is there anybody else who does this? Many charities or NGOs support a singular marginalised group through, say, elevating their voice, through training or whatever it is that they do.

Jane: Well, it's a big point you raise there. Generally, a charity looks at a particular target group that they feel requires the support of that charity for one reason or another. Global Generation doesn't do that. We do the opposite. We remove what might define a particular community. We say, no, there isn't that definition, we are all in this together because we are all human in a way.

I have to say, my colleagues didn't always see eye to eye on this. I always felt that it was fundamental to who we are; otherwise, we're just going to create more marginalisation. I had to go on a bit of a learning journey myself to realise how to explain it. In reality, there are some groups that we give extra support to so that we create a level playing field. I realised we had to do that, but I really didn't like it

1.07 : [next page] - View of Skip Garden from classroom staircase with Ali Conning-Rowland's Evaporation Coolstore in the foreground, Chris Dembinski's Hall of 100 Hands on the left and Rachael Taylor's Glass House Lantern in the background.

27

JK JR

when colleagues said, 'Oh, well we can't have them because they're a private school.' I would say no, they have needs in just the same way and we always should be open.

Sometimes I think people wanted to work with more marginalised groups, and there was pressure from the funding bodies to do that as well. But we stood our ground. Things have shifted and we found our way with it.

I remember years ago going and seeing a Chickenshed theatre production – you know who they are probably. The play was based on an Anita Roddick book, and it was performed at the Royal Opera House. I found the whole experience ecstatic. There were people of all different abilities all working together at the opera house, in this grand setting. And it released this X factor. You feel that in nature when you've got a flourishing ecosystem: it's not one-dimensional, it's mixed, but then something is released that's bigger than the whole.

It is that spark of something that always enlivens me. It can't be taught, but it can be caught. You can feel it.

I can still recall working in the old Skip Garden. I remember a group of older Camden residents and a group from Frank Barnes School and they were all working together. We were building the pizza oven and working with the bees and there was some building work going on. I wasn't directly involved on the day. I remember stepping out of the little office, which was upstairs, I remember up above the coolstore at the time, and it had that same electrical atmosphere. And I thought, this is how the

1.08 : Working on-site.
1.09 : Volunteer builders upcycling coffee bags for the Evaporation Coolstore.

Chapter 1 | Ecology + Leadership

1.10 : Facade detail of the Evaporation Coolstore.

JK   JR

world should be. So I guess there's a kind of activism involved in that in terms of wanting to dismantle walls and the glass cages and the divisions we put between people. We are a relational species, and we live in a relational universe, and that really should be our modus operandi.

Lots of amazing things came out of the modernist perspective, don't get me wrong, and we needed separation for science to flourish. But perhaps one of the things we have to do is kaleidoscope it all together again for that, that X factor to happen.

Jan: Tell me about King's Cross and the Skip Garden and also the founding days of Global Generation.

Jane: I have told you about Rise Phoenix and the camps in Pertwood. The camps were very successful, but the organisation eventually said, 'Jane, you are trying to turn us into an environmental organisation.' I said, no problem, we will set up a charity to run the camps. That was in 2004. They kept coming and doing camps with us and when they closed eventually, they left us money.

Well, we did the campsite and that was the foundation. And then we wanted to work in London. One of our first projects was with Charlie Green who set up The Office Group. He had a building in Gray's Inn Road. Charlie thought that something special could happen on the roof of his building. He was probably thinking of elegant white furniture. Anyway, I met with him and said, what about getting people involved? We were working with a group of young people who had been in prison in west London. I didn't think it was really what he had in mind, but he was up for it, so we got involved.

1.11 : Students presenting their architectural models to the client in the yurt.
1.12 : Relying on volunteer help to build their designs taught the students to engage others in their work, a skill not traditionally taught at architecture school.

1.13 : Lunch and Learning at the Skip Garden. The Garden grows community by bringing together those living, learning and working in King's Cross.

Londoners Making London

1.14 : Building the Glass House Lantern. Traditionally, architectural education rewards individual excellence. Building the Skip Garden required students to co-ordinate and collaborate.

Chapter 1 | Ecology + Leadership

JK   JR

I remember we got a load of recycled poo pellets and recycled glass from Canary Wharf and logs from Hampstead Heath and we created a rooftop garden. We later found a stag beetle there; I think it was the only rooftop in London that harboured an ancient woodland species.

So we did that and we did a number of other rooftop projects. At that time, I met Roger Madelin. He came and he famously said business and activism doesn't have to be either end of the spectrum, and I love what you are doing here. And from that moment, I loved him. I would go and hear him speak, and sometimes I'd catch him in the break and we'd have a chat.

We were working with schools in Somerstown at the time and he let us store some soil in King's Cross, on a site that eventually became the Skip Garden, but we didn't know that at the time. One time, when I saw Roger at a talk again, I said, what about creating gardens on the back of lorries, and then we can move them? It was Paul Richens, our first gardener, who came up with the idea.

Roger then offered us sites in King's Cross. But how were we going to do this? Fortuitously, *The Guardian* had just moved into King's Cross and they were looking for a way to engage their staff in the local community. I remember Tim Brooks, who was managing director of *The Guardian* newspaper at the time, looking at a little drawing on grid paper of a garden coming out of a skip that Paul had done. Tim started to laugh, and he said, 'It's a brilliant thing. It's a magic thing. We just have to do this.'

1.15 : Installing the structural column for Valerie Vyvial's chicken coop.

Londoners Making London

1.16 : Yangyang Liu's drawing of the Skip Garden was a collaborative effort, with all students providing digital models of their structures.

Chapter 1 | Ecology + Leadership

37

JK   JR

We had no money at the time, but we had put an application in for this Big Lottery grant. I got wind that we were to be one of the beacon projects, but we needed to secure matching funds. *The Guardian* came on board and ended up providing the matching funds. We built the first Skip Garden with *The Guardian*'s leadership team, young women from a refuge in Camden and secondary school students. It was again a real mix of people. I remember Zak Nur, one of our young generators. He said, 'Not only have we created a garden, but we have also created a living atmosphere'. The garden was humming. There were about 50 people working on the build and that became, in a way, emblematic of how we would work from then on.

And then we were in that garden, and then we moved the skips to another garden on York Way. And when we were set to move again; it was your colleague Julia King who kept emailing me. We had not had a fantastic experience with universities. They can be bureaucratic and complicated. I wasn't holding my breath that a lot would come of the partnership. I did not respond to her immediately. But she kept trying, and I thought, this woman, she's nice, she's persistent. So I decided to meet her and instantly liked her. And then of course I met you. You came to one of our Lunch and Learning events. I remember thinking, you guys really are prepared to make the time to get to know us. That then was a big step for us, because from a design level and through the involvement of architecture students and their ideas, it all became a lot more interesting. It was very exciting what they came up with. And then that threaded through to the subsequent projects.

JK   JR

Jan: I remember bringing a friend to the Skip Garden, a very good architect, Peter Barber. He's a real visionary. He said, 'So this is all going to go?' and I said, yes we are going to move on eventually. And he said, 'That's such a shame, you should not let them take it away.' And I said, this is not really how it works. If it were permanent, we would not have had the opportunity to do this project in the first place. And secondly, building the garden together is what's important. You should see what happens, when it moves. Hundreds of people are mobilised to help. They all come and bring their diggers and their gloves, and their tools and the garden moves and people work together. I don't know if he understood that.

Jane: Alongside this, we've found a way to embed more permanence in the charity too. When you have 23 staff, it's stressful to move the whole organisation and all our programmes. You have to find a way to do both. Meanwhile has become such a thing now. Did I tell you about my sister? She is working on this light rail project in Auckland. They have urbanists working with them and she said they all talk about meanwhile gardens. And she said to them, 'Jane might use another term, actually.' I feel our gardens are permanent, really. They've got longevity, but they're moving.

Jan: That's amazing, isn't it? What matters is the legacy that is left and the memories that people take home. That make your projects much more permanent than if they were actually there for ever.

Jane: It's not just the things we have done, it's the stories that have been told about the work. I was thinking about this the other

Chapter 1 | Ecology + Leadership

1.17 : Rachael Taylor and David Eland working out
the construction details for the Glass House Lantern.
Design challenges at the Skip Garden are solved
through both making and drawing.

39

1.18 : Charlie Redman's kinetic Welcome Shelter.

Chapter 1 | Ecology + Leadership

Londoners Making London

JK   JR

day, as we are beginning our project here in New Zealand, and I was talking about it with someone who's going to help us build the composting toilet. The benefit of using old materials is that they all carry stories with them. When you walk around any of our gardens, there are lots of stories about what they are made of and who has made them.

There is an eco-philosopher called Freya Mathews. She talks about the modernist paradigm and how it was grinding down everything, all materiality to a neutral substrate. She wrote a piece also about something that had been made out of upcycled materials. You could say that the story sphere is still present, it's not been ground down into this uniform anonymous thing. You can see why people do that, that anonymisation, because then it becomes their own. But if you're trying to create a garden of a thousand hands, you want to be able to show those hands in as many different ways as possible, whether it's the person who's given you the windows or the sleepers.

Jan: Tell me about the challenges and the moments of breakthrough.

Jane: In a way it's not for the fainthearted, this process, but I think there's light-touch ways one can live one's way into it. And as you and I have often said, the planning process doesn't lend itself to this. Often there have been moments of real worry. The usual question is: 'How are we going pay for it?' There's always a worry. The classic one, which I wrote about in my book, in the last chapter, moving to the Story Garden, was very stressful because we were a bigger charity. We were suddenly working with the British Library, a well-known institution.

1.19 : Refurbishing the windows for the Glass House Lantern. Window donations came from many places, connecting people from across the UK to Rachael's building.
1.20 : Sewing coffee bags for the Evaporation Coolstore.

42

Chapter 1 | Ecology + Leadership

1.21 : The Glass House Lantern illuminated at night.

43

JK JR

We had a board of trustees who very much liked the outcomes of what we were doing but weren't intimately involved with the process of how we got there. They got understandably quite worried about the risks. We worked in a very different way, more collaboratively. We are primarily women and there was no single person heading up the charge for the move. I can remember a meeting where they had brought in a quantity surveyor who was telling me that what we wanted to do would cost a hundred thousand pounds. Yet, we had done all this three times before and had set aside ten thousand pounds for the move. And it was one of the few times I stood up to them and just said at the top of my voice, no, no, no, because they would just rip the heart out of the organisation to try and get us to do it their way. It would have been suicide financially, philosophically and socially, which is why I refused. Over the course of the following three months, three of them stepped away. And we managed to do what we'd outlined and what they had costed at one hundred thousand pounds for just two thousand. And again, lots of people got involved. And then, as you know, lots of people came out of the woodwork and got involved in the build of the Story Garden as had been the case with the Skip Garden, and as will happen with the Paper Garden.

Of course, things do not always go to plan. I remember the roundhouse in the Story Garden: Central St Martin's did the designs and were going to build it, but they never finished it. Then one of the construction companies stepped up and did a wonderful job and did all sorts of extra things and built the other structures too. I mean Jan, you as an architect, I don't think many architects would've worked like you worked. It has

1.22 : Interior of the chicken coop.
1.23 : [ibid]

Chapter 1 | Ecology + Leadership

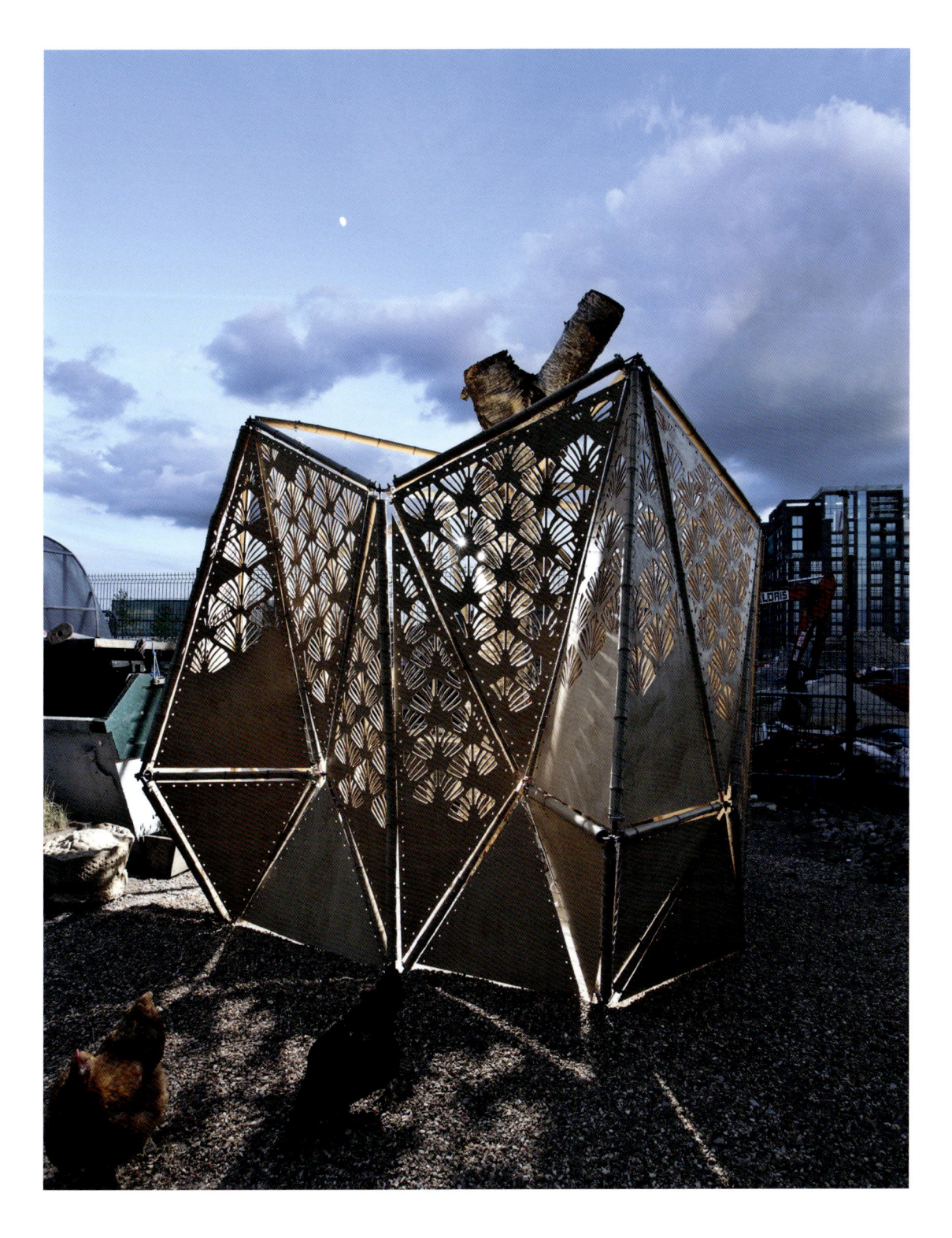

1.24 : Chicken coop lit at night.

Londoners Making London

1.25 : Even though the Skip Garden was eventually taken down to make place for development, its legacy lives on at the new Story Garden behind the British Library.

Chapter 1 | Ecology + Leadership

JK   JR

required having a lot of faith, but also having backup plans like, okay, if this doesn't work, we can scale down. We can operate out of the polytunnel. Financially, we never actually put anything at risk. And that's important, because a charity cannot work in debt. We prepared our team, people needed to know what they were in for. It wouldn't suit everybody, but when it works, it's pure magic.

Those were some of the difficult times. We worked on it together, the Story Garden. We had to push those plans through perhaps faster than was ideal, which meant we all didn't really understand them fully. But we just had to, and the British Library wanted us. We had to have something that was attractive enough to show the community. It took a bit to then open that process up in a way that we'd all hoped. Sometimes it takes a bit of stumbling and bumbling to open up that truly collaborative process. I don't really trust things that are totally smooth anymore. Even things that are very well planned – life isn't like that, and things are done by people.

Jan: You've devised a very personal methodology of storytelling, writing, making, planting and cooking together to overcome barriers and build community. You've now moved to New Zealand. What advice did you give those that are succeeding you in London?

Jane: Find a way to do it in your own shoes. Things don't always go smoothly; they can go bumpy. Get curious about those bumps and those edges and take time to pause and stop and find those little pockets or moments of silence.

Jan: Thank you, Jane.

Sitopia Farm w/ Chloë Dunnett

2020 – Present
London, Welling, DA16

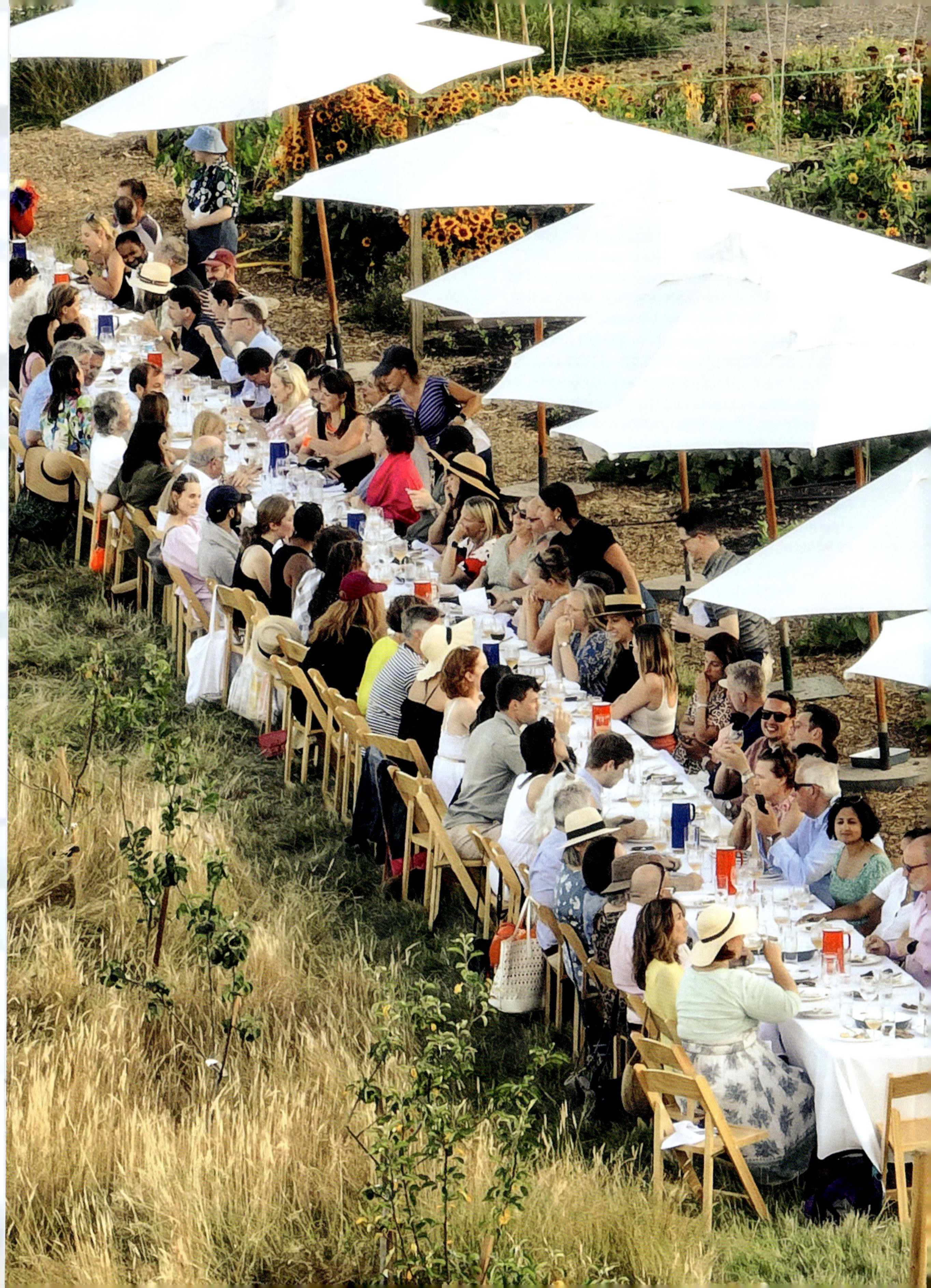

Londoners Making London

1.29 : Chloë harvesting flowers in the polytunnel. Combining vegetable production with flower production is a key element of Sitopia's business model.

Chapter 1 | Ecology + Leadership

JK   CD

problems. If we farm in a different way, if we consume and eat in a different way, if we structure the system differently, it could be transformative. Food brings joy. It's how we come together as humans, around good food.

That's the broader vision. I wanted to take direct action. I think we also urgently need governmental policy change. I wanted to be part of the change we need to see on the ground, to help show what's possible in a short space of time, and also to encourage the spread of more farms like ours. We cannot change the food system by ourselves, but more and more of us are starting to make a difference, and part of what we're about is advocacy and spreading the word to help engender the wider policy and system change that's so desperately needed.

Jan: Your farm has a very particular business model, different from other farms. Is it really a scalable model? And is it reliable? You rely on others to help. What do people gain from being involved?

Chloë: I am not sure I'd necessarily say it's that different. How do you see it being different from other farms?

Jan: For starters, most farms are run for profit. Your farm produces food, is concerned about well-being and is also a vehicle for direct action and advocacy and to promote system change.

Chloë: Yes, when you put it like that it becomes interesting. Smaller-scale organic farms are different, actually. I think there are a lot of younger people coming into the movement. A lot of them are motivated

1.30 : Growing varied crops that flower at different times supports biodiversity.

Londoners Making London

1.31 : Sitopia Farm from above. Creating a beautiful space helps to engage others in the farm's mission.

JK   CD

by politics, the food system crisis and the desire for change. And not-for-profit does not mean that we don't sell. We absolutely need to in order to cover our costs, and we also want to demonstrate how small urban and peri-urban farms can be viable. Our model is that we aim to cover our costs by selling our vegetables and flowers, supplemented by other income-generating activities such as hosting events, courses and, in the future, much, much more. The priority is to grow proper volumes of food. We do offer discounts for people on low incomes for our veg-box schemes and make regular donations to local food projects and charities to improve accessibility.

Our initial capital infrastructure costs were covered by a Mayor's grant and crowdfunding. We raised around £70k through that route – which was mind-blowing, really, starting with nothing. We had 400 people, many of them local, who backed us. I hope to secure some more outside funding to help pay for the infrastructure that we need to move beyond our start-up phase: to enable us to store and pack food more efficiently, provide better facilities for volunteers and host a much wider range of activities.

Jan: You don't just grow food, you grow flowers too. Why not concentrate on food?

Chloë: Growing flowers was initially experimental. It has become a success in a number of ways. We want the space to be beautiful because we want people to come and connect to the land, and each other. The flowers really help with that. Society, or at least the market, seems to value flowers more than vegetables – they can generate more profit and help cross-

JK   CD

subsidise the vegetables. The social and environmental impact of conventionally grown flowers is also particularly poor. Something like 88 per cent of cut flowers in the UK are grown abroad, often on the other side of the world, in heated and chemically treated greenhouses tended to by workers working in appalling conditions, then often wrapped in plastic, refrigerated, flown to the UK, wrapped in cellophane and sold out of season. Finally, it's important to have biodiversity on the farm, and the flowers contribute to that.

Going back to the business model, our aim is to be as efficient as possible, trying to capture as much value as we can by selling a large percentage directly to our customers whilst also selling to local businesses and restaurant wholesalers. We are still experimenting, figuring out what is viable, what makes sense. Having a diversity of crops is part of that, and it also gives us resilience in the context of climate change. The nature of working with nature is that it is unpredictable. Having different outlets for our produce and different kinds of customers also helps us spread the risk and improve resilience. And it's also a way of reaching different people.

We have a big event on Saturday. It's by a Californian organisation, Outstanding in the Field. It's essentially an outdoor dining experience. They source the food as locally as possible, they use proper crockery and chefs, and afterwards everything is taken away. We get a fee for that. And companies undertake team awaydays on the farm and we get paid for our time as hosts. People have a great time. They feel useful working outdoors. We have also had a couple of filming events. So we are trying to be a bit

1.32 : [next page] - Dining event at Sitopia Farm.

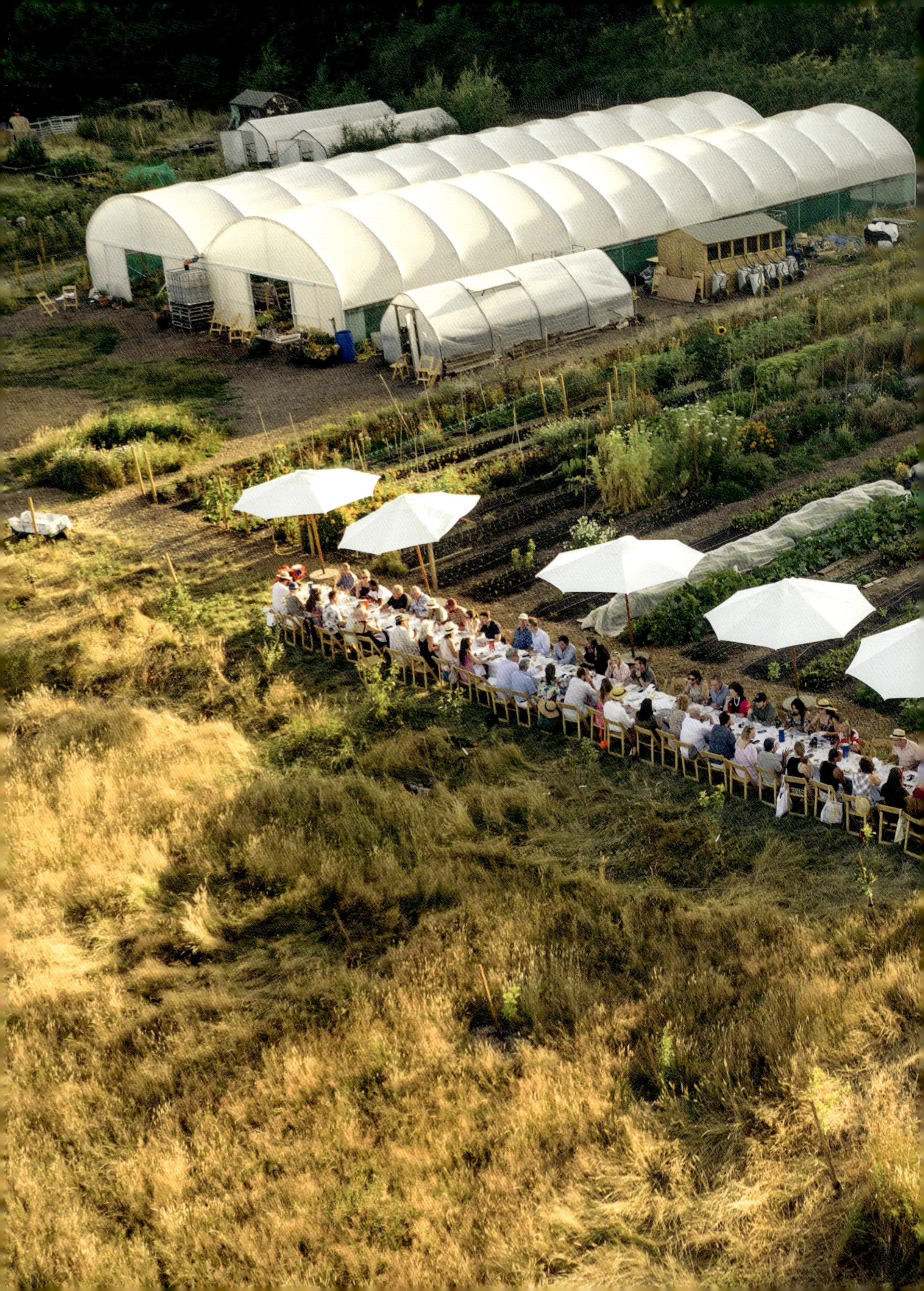

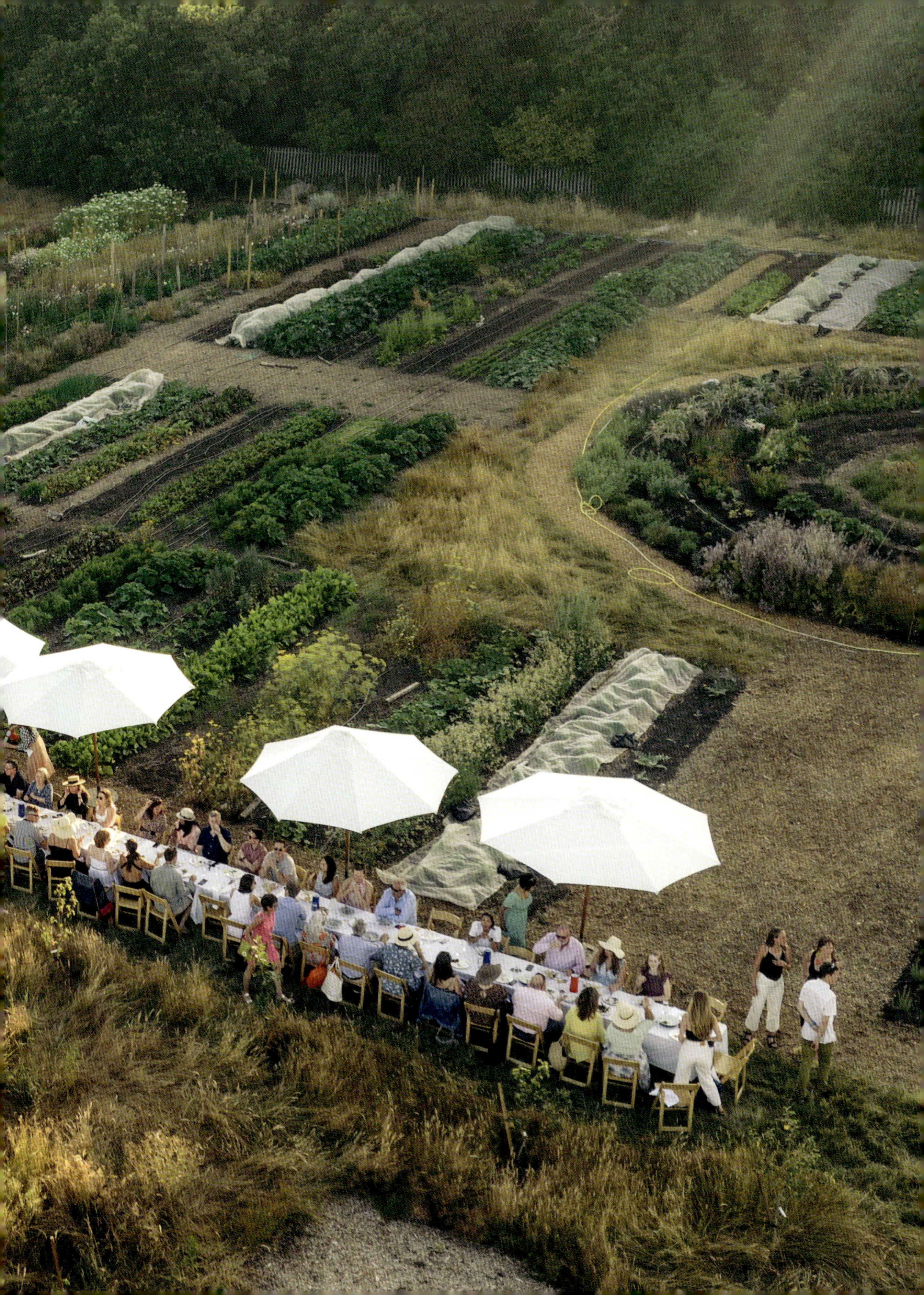

1.33 : Chloë with organic vegetables grown at Sitopia Farm. Reducing the distance from field to fork is key to reducing the environmental and social cost of farming.

Chapter 1 | Ecology + Leadership

JK   CD   JK   CD

innovative. It's a very different business model: from monoculture to multiculture. We have done a bit of outreach work with schools. I'd love to do more of that. I'd love to explore social prescribing, work with ex-offenders. For them – as with everyone – it could be quite therapeutic.

Jan: I have a friend, he runs a community garden opposite Wandsworth prison. They used to do a lot of work with prisoners, but because the prison system has been privatised it's much harder. There's no interest from the prison in giving access to their inmates or those in rehabilitation.

Tell me a bit about the challenges along the way – and the moments of breakthrough and delight. How much of where you are now is the result of luck and coincidence, and how much of it is the result of determination and planning? You got the land. Was there ever a moment, when you first got onto the land, when you thought, God, this is a big task that I have taken on here?

Chloë: Sure. I think probably every day I have a mixture of all these feelings. On the one hand, this was the plan and I spent quite a lot of time researching and developing the business, bringing people with the right skills together to execute the plan and to get advice. We absolutely stand on the shoulders of giants, learning from other farmers and other pioneer entrepreneurs. All that said, I feel incredibly lucky to have found this bit of land. I have had so much support from so many different people, and it does feel a bit magical – serendipity or something. I remember, early on, I thought, I really need someone who is good at design or marketing. I knew I needed a better logo

and a website. And literally the next day I got an email out of the blue from a guy who worked in design and had tens of thousands of followers on Instagram. He was really interested in regenerative agriculture and he just said, 'I imagine you are a bit busy, do you need any help?' We ended up having a long conversation and he put me in touch with a designer, Risa Sano from Mentsen, who has since done a huge amount of pro bono design work for us. You know, there are lots of examples of things like that.

We have had several hundred volunteers give up their time entirely for free to help create the farm, and they still come. We absolutely benefit from that. And the generosity of Woodlands Farm in the first place (and now). I do slightly believe that you make your luck happen to an extent. During the last year I was at the farm six or seven days a week. It was really consuming. I am now nine months pregnant and I have been trying not to do quite so much. I was working at the farm until a week and a bit ago. The last week was a bit more challenging – I couldn't do my shoes up. My maternity cover, Rachel, is now working full time at the farm having taken a sabbatical from a very well-paid job in a sustainability consultancy. It's not a big salary at the farm, but she believes in this.

Farming is hard at the best of times; there are slim margins, particularly with the kind of farming we do. We are competing with a system where the cost of food is misleading. Food prices in supermarkets do not reflect the true cost of food. In the short term it might be quicker and more profitable to spread chemicals to prevent pests, spread fertilisers, etc. We are not doing those things because it's not good for

61

JK CD

the environment or our health in the long run. But that's not reflected in the price of food, so someone else is picking the tab up somewhere. That's the taxpayers and ultimately future generations. So to make a living when you are competing with the dominant system is hard. I barely took a salary the first year and had to rent out my flat on Airbnb and just not spend very much. But that's my choice. This year we are hopefully doing better; we are doing better already.

Jan: Your farm is not just about farming. It has an educational remit; you have ecological commitments, and then there's the running of the business. Are you a brilliant generalist, or do you feel you are winging it sometimes?

Chloë: Everything is new to me. I am new to running a business, new to running a farm, so I am learning all the time. It's both utterly brilliant and also challenging. Of course there are days when I wonder, am I capable of this? But not once have I thought that this isn't the right thing to be doing. This is what I am doing. It feels 100 per cent like this is what we need to do. We need more farms like ours. We need to change the system.

I gave Rachel a present last week, a brilliant book called *Letters to a Young Farmer.* It's a compilation of letters from incredible writers. And one of the things that's clear is there is a whole breadth of skills needed in this profession. So you need to be a generalist – as well as a specialist. It's probably like any entrepreneur running a small business. You need a grasp of the finances, the marketing, the sales, the communications, and then there are the volunteers, and you are trying to have a

JK CD

social impact too. I suppose that suits me. I have always enjoyed doing lots of different things. But I also rely on others to help. On our board we have a range of skills and experiences which help me; for example, Dan has worked on huge regeneration projects, Anna is a lawyer, Milton has experience of developing a small business. Alice is an organic farmer with over 20 years of experience. I employ a part-time bookkeeper/accountant. In my previous life I was a civil servant. Being a civil servant is often about managing big projects and programmes and not being the expert but working with the experts. It's not about doing it all yourself, it's about bringing in a wide variety of people with different skills to get things done. It's delivering through others.

Jan: What do you think we can learn from Sitopia Farm about cities and urbanism and how we live in cities?

Chloë: One of the really important things about Sitopia Farm is that we are in the city. It comes with its own challenges, but urban farms are so important. We benefit from a much-reduced distance between field and fork. There is land available in London and in other cities. The University of Sheffield, for example, has done a lot of research on this using geospatial mapping. You don't need a lot of land to grow a lot of food. Being in the city, we are intimately connected. In the food system, there is such a disconnect between production and consumption. I have a friend who lives around here and grew up in London, and he said to me, I didn't realise that tomatoes are seasonal. Why would he have known? When you go to the supermarket, everything is there all year round, wrapped in plastic, flown in from

Chapter 1 | Ecology + Leadership

JK   CD

wherever. You are not aware what's gone into that. It's not something you think about. And I think that contributes to the situation we are in. Connecting consumers and production is an important part of changing that picture. With our farm, we are within reach of millions of people. And they can come and be part of it. People come and visit or volunteer and it blows their mind. We get children who thought they hated salad and who now realise that it actually tastes of something because it's a totally different experience from what you get in the supermarket.

Our vision is to have a network of urban and peri-urban farms feeding the city. I was listening to the radio this morning and they were discussing how this heatwave that we are having will become a normal occurrence. They talk of us having the weather of Barcelona in 2050. There is lots of evidence that productive green spaces, no-dig and no-till farming can help reduce carbon emissions and flooding, and green spaces can reduce the temperature in the city. I think it's very primal for all of us to have a connection with the land and where our food comes from, something we have lost. With the food system that we have, we could have a massive farm just next to where we live and yet actually get our food from somewhere completely different – the other side of the country or another country entirely.

Jan: What's stopping us? Organic urban gardens in Cuba have been around for decades. Beijing produces a significant proportion of its produce within city limits. Why not us?

1.34 : View across the farm.

Londoners Making London

1.35 : Harvesting flowers.

1.36 : Harvesting vegetables.

JK   CD

Chloë: There are many small community gardens in London. They serve a really important purpose, but you cannot feed very many people from a small community garden. Of course there used to be larger market gardens, in Paris and also in London. Limiting factors are the competing pressures over land, the cost of land in London, the lack of prioritisation by government and the failure to realise the urgency with which we must adjust our priorities.

I have spoken to quite a few people and organisations who had been thinking about growing food, but they did not know where to begin. And then there is a bit of a disconnect between those in control of land and the people with the capacity and desire to actually farm it. I think there is scope for bringing them together. And I think we need a more enabling policy framework, whether that's at a local or national government level. We need more support for new entrants into farming, training, start-up finance.

We have the highest consumption of ultra-processed food in Europe here in the UK. It's no accident that we suffer from the highest rate of obesity.

Our government of course supposedly has the great opportunity of Brexit to reform our agricultural subsidy system and to support more nature-friendly farming rather than just paying farmers for acreage. But there's hardly any mention of food in policy. The vast majority of the recommendations made in the governmental food system review led by Henry Dimbleby recently are not being taken forward. Yet, we need to change because the dominant agrochemical farming system under which most of our food is produced and sold is not doing us or the environment any good.

Jan: Thank you, Chloë.

Chapter 1 | Ecology + Leadership

1.37 : The food and flower stall at the farm sells straight to the consumer, realising maximum value for the farm.

Thornhill Library w/ Emily Bohill + Kate Slotover

2017 – Present

London, Islington, N1

Chapter 1 | Ecology + Leadership

1.37 : The food and flower stall at the farm sells straight to the consumer, realising maximum value for the farm.

67

2 / Enterprise + Learning

This chapter tells the stories of three projects: a school library, a vocational academy and a housing project. The programme of two of them is about education and manufacturing. The reason they have been put together in one chapter, however, is not the function of the resulting buildings, but the recognition that learning and enterprise are central to how they were conceived and realised. In the Church Grove interview, I learned about embedding learning and enterprise in project development, which is why I have included it in this chapter. The real impact of all three projects is not the delivery of new facilities, but the reinvention of the process that leads to the creation of these spaces in the first place.

Urban theorist Charles Landry distinguishes between the 'reflexive city and the unreflexive city'. Success is contingent on reflection and learning being hard-wired into the planning process. Progress will falter without it. He writes:

> 'The most engaged, forward-looking and successful cities harness their collective imagination and learning. They reflect on their experience and that of others. A learning city is constantly on the lookout, searching out examples of success and failure, always questioning why this is so. It benchmarks itself to relevant other cities to get a grip on how well it is evolving. Thus, it understands itself – it is a 'reflexive city', always self-improving and aware. It has embedded a culture of learning into the genetic code of its city.'

Innovation is traditionally linked to technology or design. Many urbanists recognise that the spaces in a city are largely the result of the processes that we have established to create them. To advance, that process needs to change. Landry describes the reinvention of city-making processes as 'creative bureaucracy'. A central objective of 'creative bureaucracy' is the adoption of a 'human perspective'. Most bureaucrats, Landry explains, are in their job 'because they want to make a difference in big and small ways'.

Thornhill Library, the Tailoring Academy and Church Grove are all a response to the failure of existing systems. Government funding cuts compromising children's education prompted the building of Thornhill Library, the Tailoring Academy is a response to unsustainable and unethical practices in garment manufacturing, and Church Grove responds to the affordability crisis of homes in London. Each project establishes new processes, from first principles.

Innovation is often associated with the work of experts. In this chapter, innovation is the result of people with no previous knowledge in the field rebuilding a process from the ground up. All three tell of the hardship that they have encountered along the way. However, it is this defiance of challenge and adversity that has built communities and led them to formalise as the resilient organisations that they are today. Coming from the outside and inhabiting what Emily Bohill calls 'the crack in the system' is allowing them to address systemic deficiencies. Their only tool at the outset was a clear objective and the ability to mobilise others to their cause.

Setbacks are an inherent ingredient of innovation. Anurag Verma and Jon Broome explain in their interview how each crisis and each setback has strengthened their organisation. By assigning a monetary value to risk, many institutions are unwittingly stifling innovation. Mariana Mazzucato and Rosie Collington's book *The Big Con* explains how risk aversion and indecisiveness are weakening institutions, which increasingly rely on consultancy rather than on the 'cleverness, ingenuity, aspiration, motivation, imagination and creativity' of their people.

The business support programme delivered by social enterprise Meanwhile Space, the community interest company managing Blue House Yard, is set up to give businesses the best chance to succeed. This is achieved by creating a safe environment where they are allowed to fail – without long-term financial consequences. The theory is that reducing the repercussions of failing encourages risk-taking whilst also shortening the lag between failure and a smarter, more informed restart (and ultimate success).

All three organisations discussed in this chapter have grown out of a particular project at hand. But they also have an ambition to build a legacy beyond a singular project. The Thornhill Foundation and Run Kids Run, both of which grew out of the library project, are now enabling educational activities in schools across and beyond London. Through mentoring and research, Fashion Enter is enabling others and the wider industry to embrace sustainable, UK-based production. And The Rural Urban Synthesis Society (RUSS) has set up the RUSS School, with four modules aimed at making community-led housing available to communities across the UK.

Thornhill Library w/ Emily Bohill + Kate Slotover

2017 – Present

London, Islington, N1

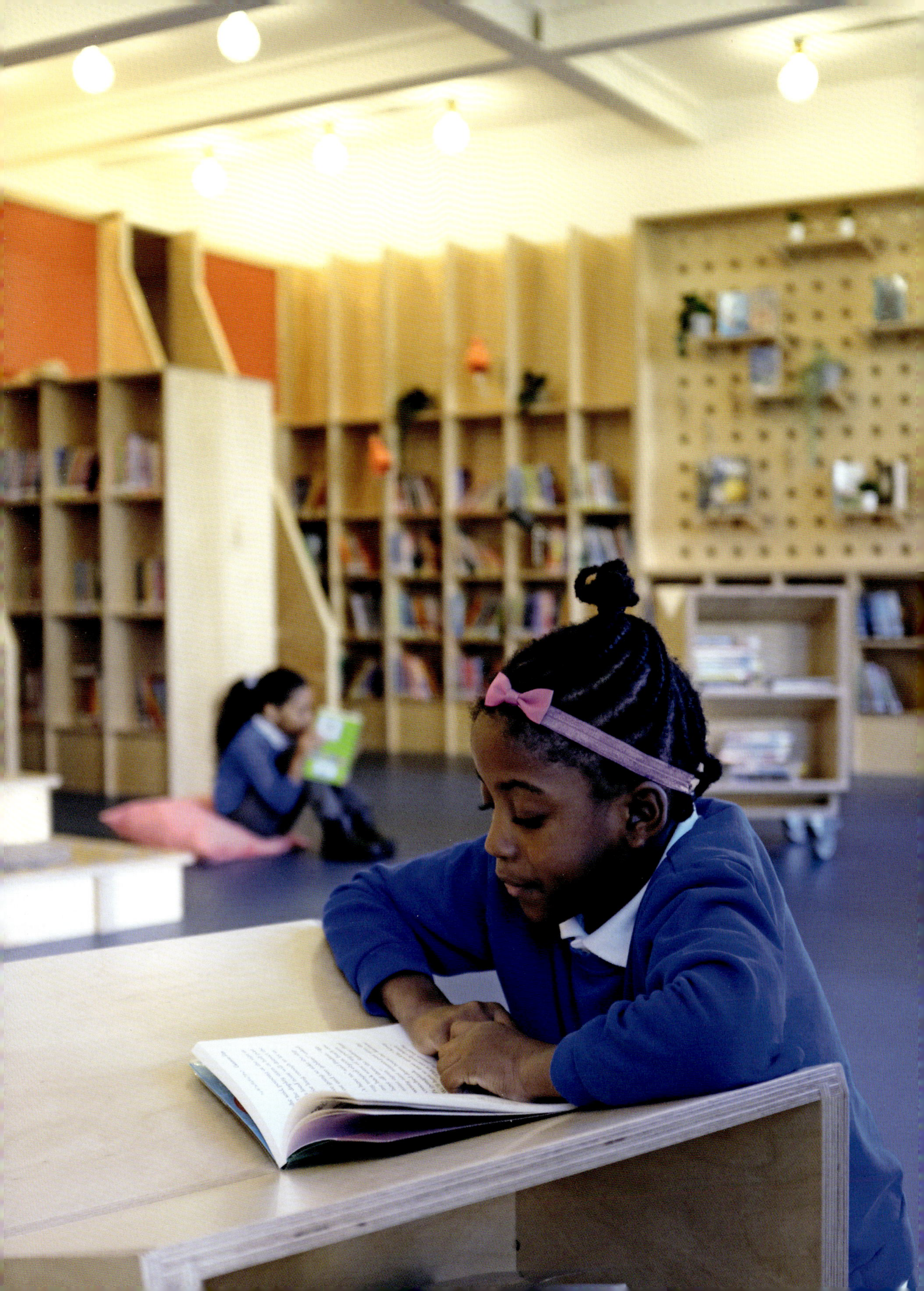

About

When parents at Thornhill Primary School in North London realised how government-imposed funding cuts would impact their children's education, they decided to take action. Plans to build a new school library galvanised the community's resolve to step up and support the school's educational mission. Thornhill Primary School wants pupils to develop a love for learning. The library project was integral to achieving this mission, empowering children as young as four to be the authors of their own learning experiences in an inspirational environment. The new library makes use of a former undercroft to create a multifunctional space for browsing, readings, performance and role play.

The project went on to mobilise the entire school community: teachers gave up their weekend to participate in a costumed fun run, pupils organised cake and lemonade sales, parents and carers secured sponsorship from alumni and community members, local businesses donated for the school raffle and famous family friends performed for free in a sold-out comedy gig.

The impact that the new library has had on pupils' attainment will only be fully understood in time. What is clear already is that the library project served as a catalyst which unleashed a much more ambitious mission to improve children's education. In the context of continuing funding shortfalls and stubborn inequality – in 2019 Islington had the tenth highest level of income deprivation affecting children in England – parents across Islington's primary schools are now sharing resources and knowledge about the Thornhill approach.

To formalise methods and secure the legacy for forthcoming pupil and parent generations, two charities were set up. The Thornhill Foundation has gone on to fund other projects at Thornhill Primary School, including the creation of a dance studio and an outdoor physical education parkour. Run Kids Run is a national charity organising mini marathons for primary school children and their parents to raise funds for school projects.

Kate Slotover, Emily Bohill and Jo Michaelides were instrumental in engaging others and driving the project. With her background in graphic design, Kate succeeded in articulating the objectives of Thornhill's campaign. Emily's focus on tangible outcomes and ability to make Thornhill's success a concern for the entire community leveraged unheard-of support from both individuals in the immediate community and organisations and partners from across London.

2.01 : [previous page] - Pupil reading. Having the choice of what to read and also of where to read is an important part of the educational experience at Thornhill.

Chapter 2 | Enterprise + Learning

JK   EB + KS   JK   EB + KS

2.02 : Kate Slotover and Emily Bohill with Thornhill pupils.

Jan: Kate and Emily, thank you for taking the time to speak to me about your work at Thornhill Primary School. Can you tell me about the school itself first? What makes it different? What is your connection with it, and what was that very moment when you both thought, 'right, something's got to happen'.

Emily: Thornhill is a really special school. There's a hashtag Thornhill Together, which sums up why. And there's a community that's really involved and cares and that's also quite ambitious. But ambitious for everyone. Quite often at a school you find parents who are ambitious for their own kids. What marks my experience at Thornhill is that people have high hopes for the whole community. It's not just about getting their little Timothy the best education, it's about getting the whole community the best education.

We often talk about the crack in the system and the Leonard Cohen poem saying that there's a crack in everything; that's how the light gets in. For us the crack was the government cutbacks. The pressure on the school could have meant that it reduced enriching activities for the kids. But through the defiance and sheer determination of Jenny Lewis, the headteacher, and the senior leadership team including Louise Ryer, we went the other way. When Jo Michaelides set up the Foundation, it was a means to connect the community to the school and find a way to fund ambitious projects that the school wanted to deliver …

Kate: … projects that the school wouldn't have been able to deliver with its own budget. We should say, as parents, when your children start at school, you are invested in it for seven years. If you have more than one child, it's longer than that. And as a result, particularly in primary schools, there's this amazing hub of people who have all these incredible skills, professional backgrounds and expertise, and who are all united by wanting the best for their children and all the children in that school.

What was brilliant about Jo Michaelides, who was a parent and a parent governor, was that original insight and vision for a more formal fundraising structure that would help us to harness what the parent community were able to do. And when Emily came along, she brought her own twist.

Emily: I was amazed at how welcoming and open our school was to parents getting involved. And I just thought, charity begins at home; your school is your kid's second home. It was a no-brainer, really, to get involved and to try and make things happen. You are engaging with parents who of course have open ears to helping out. I think what Thornhill did really well was to

75

JK   EB + KS

engage the wider community, including people who did not have kids at the school. A letter went out. We had all our children do mail drop and deliver the letters. The letter started with, 'Good schools make good communities.' That was a really powerful sentence and I really think that struck a chord. You realise this school is on the doorstep of your house and ask yourself, 'What can I do to help?'

Islington is a very diverse area. Alongside great wealth we have great deprivation. I think there was an awareness of that and maybe a sense of responsibility amongst people who might have thought: 'I don't have kids at Thornhill, but I have a really nice house in Barnsbury and I walk past the school every day.'

Jan: Kate, what was that moment for you, when you thought 'I should get involved'?

Kate: I think it was the personal connection. There were some very dynamic figures in the Parent Teacher Association (PTA) at the time. Jo in particular had a more ambitious vision and I think a more acute sense because of her role as parent-governor. I think I was inspired and I was very impressed at that kind of energy and ambition and drive. I knew also that I had skills that could help. I'm a graphic designer. I realised that a big part of realising that vision was going to be communications. I realised that it was going to be about presenting something that looked authoritative and convincing, something that was going to persuade people. You need a bit of marketing skill. It's all very well sending out letters, but how do you make someone actually want to read that letter? How do you make them pick it up? There

JK   EB + KS

are things you can do. I think I saw that. I had a skillset that could help. I remember slightly naively in an early meeting raising my hand and just saying, 'Well, if there's anything I can do?'

Looking back, I think you need to harness that interest and enthusiasm and engagement that parents have when they first come to the school and when they realise that their children will spend the next seven years together.

Emily: I think for me it was that level of professionalism. I remember at drop-off talking to you at the gates about the library and about the plans and the timescale, when you walked out just having had a meeting with the senior leadership team. And I remember thinking, goodness me, they are that advanced, they've got a professional architect on the case. For me that was a turning point. I thought, okay if we can get that money, this will happen. £270k seemed like an enormous amount of money to raise.

Kate: It was more money than had ever been raised for any other project at school.

Emily: And since then, Thornhill has raised more money and we have delivered on the library, on the STEM [science, technology, engineering and mathematics] lab, the computer space, the dance studio, the early years space and the nursery.

Jan: Kate, what is it that you actually did to make all this happen? Once you were invested and you'd offered to do things, what was the chronology of events? You edited a poetry book, you made a film, you installed a Little Free Library …

Chapter 2 | Enterprise + Learning

2.03 : Reading at Thornhill Library is also a communal experience.

77

JK   EB + KS

Kate: It was a moment when I had a little bit more time on my hands, so I got involved in making a poetry book. I could see that it was a project that the school would have loved to have done, but it was going to be a real challenge for them to find the resources to do it, not least in terms of time. I am a book designer, and I thought this would be a really nice thing to help them achieve. My world is books and reading, and so I am very interested in that side of education. The children called the book *Climbing Trees to Touch the Stars*. To make the book we worked with the school's poet, Paul Lyalls, who has been involved with Thornhill for years. What's amazing about the book is that every single child has a poem in it, every child from that cohort is now a published poet. These children can go through the rest of their lives and say that. It was brilliant, it was inclusive, everyone was involved, everyone got something out of it.

I suppose, more generally, whenever I could identify something that I could do and that no one else was able to do, I would just try and do it. With the library, it seemed really clear that a film explaining why we needed a new library and how a new library would benefit the children would be really helpful. I know how to do filming and simple editing, so we got that done. And then further down the line the film was instrumental when we did fundraising events. It was one specific piece of work to make the film, but it felt as if it had quite a long tail throughout the campaign.

Then there was the Little Free Library. We were fundraising for the big library and I thought, wouldn't it be lovely to have a Little Free Library outside the school, on the school railings, connecting with the

JK   EB + KS

community. The idea did make us slightly nervous at the time. How would people react? Inside the school it's quite protected and regulated. It would have been very easy to do something inside, but we wanted to have it outside the school, on the street. We wanted to have it so that anyone and everyone could come and use it. And the idea was that in this way, the Little Free Library would connect to the big library.

We found a wonderful parent, Brian, who makes things. He built us the shell. And Susan Yen, another parent who is an interiors architect, thought quite carefully about how the little library would connect with the architecture of the Victorian school building. The design of our little library mirrors those tall windows and the pointed gable of the roof. The idea is that it feels like it fits in.

And then it had to be hand-painted by someone, which of course ended up being me. It was quite tricky to do it because we wanted to have the school's logo on it. The school's logo is quite detailed, with a globe in the centre and an interlinking ring of the silhouettes of children standing around it. At that point, when I was ready to lose the will to live, Susan came over and we spent the day in the shed painting together. The first night it was erected and stocked with books open for all the world, I almost went and sat in my car to keep an eye on it, I was so worried that it'd be ripped down. In fact, we discovered very quickly just how pleased people were to have such a lovely thing that's there for everyone. It's coming up to five years that it's been up. Once, one of the panes of Perspex cracked and Brian replaced it. The other day I found out that it made no. 1 on Londonist's list of favourite Little Free Libraries.

Chapter 2 | Enterprise + Learning

JK   EB + KS

          Emily: People are proud of it. They look after it. It even has its own social media account which Kate manages. Traditional libraries are sometimes difficult to access. They are not open all the time. With the Little Free Library, if you realise on a Sunday morning, oh my god, the kids have no books, you can go down. There's always something there. Thanks to Kate, Brian and Susan, we are now putting these Little Free Libraries on the gates of the other schools in Islington. One is going up at Laycock School shortly.

Jan: Emily, how were you involved? What did you do and how did it all start?

          Emily: I was new. Mikey, my eldest, was in reception and Sophie was not at school yet. There was this tentative peering over the school gates and thinking 'How can I get involved?' I was helping at the PTA initially and doing a cake sale. I remember overhearing someone who had tried one of my cakes, and let's just say it wasn't a success. I thought right, I am not a baker, I cannot contribute in that way. I heard parents speak about the Foundation. We were meeting between 8 am and 10 am once per term discussing plans for raising money, for speaking to businesses and the community and for applying for grants. I had confidence in this area because in my day job I run an executive search and advisory firm. We work with global investors, advisors, developers in the real estate and infrastructure market. I had a good sense of the challenges for this sector to connect with their local communities. I also knew about the funding restrictions that communities were experiencing. So I saw this lovely Venn diagram coming together of how maybe I could connect the dots.

JK   EB + KS

          And the connections were made through little things. I happened to meet someone at an event who introduced themselves as a Chair of a company, but also as the Chair of a foundation that funds children's education in North London, primarily in Islington. So I said, I may have a project for you. This serendipitous encounter led to Richard Reeve's Foundation giving us £20k for books for the new library.

          One of the big fundraisers we did was the Union Chapel Comedy Night with Russell Howard, Katherine Ryan and Jon Richardson, led by one of the dads at the school who had a connection to these comedians. It was an incredible night. We sold out at the Union Chapel, which has a thousand-seat capacity. We designed a corporate package and local businesses took tickets, we organised a green-room experience and took donations on the night. I think we raised £40k.

          The other idea we had was a big dinner. I am a big fan of alliteration, so we called it the Foundation's Fabulous Festive Feast. The first event was supported by the local pub, the Drapers Arms. We had 50 covers and raised around £10k. Then it became an annual fixture which has outgrown the Drapers Arms. We are now at the Hammerton Brewery, who are very generous with their support, and they have a capacity of more than 100. For the dinners we have been able to seek match funding. For every pound we raise, someone else will match it. And so, over the last couple of years, we've raised quite a bit of money that way.

          Kate: I personally wouldn't have made that leap. It's you who thought to yourself, 'Okay, we are going be making X amount, can I find

JK   EB + KS

a wealthy person who can match that?' Is it literally just that simple?

Emily: I think it all comes back to that sentence, 'Good schools make good communities.' And it's not an easy ask, but it's saying, look, we want to do all of these things, but we have a track record of delivering. So as custodians of your donation, we will look after it extremely well. The Foundation is really professionally run and I think everything that's happened with Thornhill has helped people feel confident and trust us. 'They have a plan, they have a vision, they have a good team, they're going to do it. If I back that project, whatever that project is, the school is delivering.'

I think we've really been able to evidence the impact of the work. It is now coming through in the results the school is experiencing. Thornhill has become the number one school in Islington, and there are all sorts of data to back that up.

We are really lucky. We had parents who are very well connected and well resourced. I don't think that's replicable in every school, but I think every community has it. I think the question is, 'Who are we, what have we got? What's the make-up of the school, what can you bring?' It's not about the money. It's gathering a collection of people who just make it happen. Some will write a cheque, but others will do the harder stuff, the painful stuff of making things happen. It's about creating an environment where people feel, okay, I have something to give and it's wanted and valued.

Crucially, you need more people doing less. If you just have two people doing

JK   EB + KS

everything, they get burned out, they get bitter and they then start to kill the enthusiasm of any newcomers. You need to harness the energy of the new parents by making them feel welcome. They are there to give anyway and are opening up.

Jan: We have talked about engaging funders and engaging the wider community. The real success for me is how you have been able to mobilise the school community, new parents, old parents, teachers, and the children too, of course. Can you tell me how you achieved that?

Emily: I think there was diversity to the projects that allowed people to get involved. Someone might say 'I love running, I want to get involved in Run Thornhill Run', or 'I love food, so the Festive Feast is the draw'. Or 'I love the governance aspect of it, so I want to be a trustee or a governor'. In the early days, I remember we sat down and did this big map of everything that went on at the school, from cake sales to discos, the Christmas fair, the ceilidh, to the Foundation. The big question over the top of the map was: 'How can I help?'

Jan: It's about having this big ambition, but breaking it down into chunks that people can take ownership over.

Kate: Making the ask a bit more specific is important. We're finding that if you ask people just to give their time, it's quite easy to say 'no'. Instead of saying, 'Can you give time on Friday afternoons to support the Enrichment programme', it's better if we can ask people to come in from 1 pm to 3 pm on Friday to perform a specific role, whether that's leading a class or supporting someone else as they do it. And we are saying, 'It will

Chapter 2 | Enterprise + Learning

JK   EB + KS

take two hours of your time, we'd love you to do this specific task, can you do it?' Then it becomes something that's quite hard to say 'no' to, especially if it is something that you could do.

The question is: 'What will people say yes to?' They won't say yes to a huge, overwhelming thing.

Emily: It's also showing that there's so much to do, there's enough for everyone. We should probably speak about the run. The idea came about during an exercise class organised by one of the mums. I thought, okay, why don't we just get loads of dads and mums to run the Hackney half? So I looked into that and realised, oh, it's £50 to enter, that money just goes to whoever is behind that run. I thought, let's just do a fun run ourselves. I mentioned the idea to Kate and she designed this amazing mascot and all the graphics, from the sponsorship page to the flyers. It looked like a proper event. So then I thought, well, I have to live up to that then. So that's how Run Thornhill Run was born: we would gather children and parents to do a run and we'd do it on a Sunday. We had an ambitious goal with the library, but a tangible one. We knew if we were to raise a lot of money at this event, we'd go a long way to building the library. The first run raised close to £20k, which was enormous.

Kids from nursery all the way up to year six took part, raising a pound from their granny and their neighbours. The sense of community was immense and running is really accessible, you don't need expensive kit. It felt like the very best of Thornhill, and we had huge involvement from kids and even from parents we don't normally

2.04 : The project architect Gareth Marriott defining design parameters with the pupils in assembly.

Londoners Making London

2.05 : Pupil with her dream library model. Four hundred little libray models informed the design brief for the big library.

2.06 : Pupil with his dream library model. Thornhill pupils were given a homework kit to make a model of their dream library.

Chapter 2 | Enterprise + Learning

2.07 : Pupil with her dream library model. Working with the school to integrate the design process with the regular curriculum meant that the pupils, parents and teaching staff took ownership of the library project.

83

JK	EB + KS

see, and they were there, wanting to get involved.

When organising the second run, a year later, I became involved in a network of PTAs in the area. We realised that there are all of these schools doing the same things. For instance, they were replicating Christmas fairs, and we thought, we could share equipment so we weren't buying or wasting the same things. I asked myself, will we be losing a bit of the magic of having ownership of Run Thornhill Run, or should we share its success by inviting other schools? There was a definitive debate about it. The next event raised £40k and four Islington schools were taking part. After that, we knew we were onto something that could be replicated. So I started Run Kids Run, which is a charity that puts on runs with state primary schools, and we leverage funding from local investors, developers and businesses. We had our first event in Camden in May, where five schools took part. That raised about £50k. The Stratford run is next Sunday in the Olympic Park. Then we will do Battersea, Lambeth, Wandsworth and Fulham. It's growing exponentially. And it all started at Thornhill. It's a gift from Thornhill to kids across London – which I am really proud of.

It does three things: it heightens community spirit, it gives kids a sense of amazing achievement and we commit to fund a project worth at least £5k in each participating school.

Kate: For me, the question is, how do we take this learning and experience so that other schools can benefit?

Emily: Well, we could never replicate things exactly. It really does start with sitting around a table and going, 'Okay, what have you got?' Because you'll have something.

JK	EB + KS

Jan: There was the fundraising and all the amazing initiatives that developed their own momentum and that brought their own social value. I want to come back to the library for a moment. What were the challenges along the way?

Kate: The library was brilliant, because there was such a clear need for it. The school had an old library. It was neglected, the school didn't really have the resources they needed for it. The school gave the children access to books in a corner of the classroom, but that was problematic. There was nowhere for them to be quiet with a book.

As a reader and also as a parent, I just knew instinctively how important it is that children have access to books and reading, are encouraged to feel excited about reading and inspired by books and that their peers are feeling excited and inspired. How can you make it something that they will want to do?

What we learned along the way was it wasn't going to work if a group of parents came into the school from the outside saying, 'This is what we think you should have.' That was a difficult realisation. You think, 'We'll give you something much better than what you have, it will be perfect and we'll pay for it. What's the problem?' And what you learn is, of course, there are so many really fundamental considerations that the school brings to a project like that. They need to think about resourcing and about delivering the curriculum, about how a big outside investment like this affects their own funding and budget which has to be so carefully managed. What we were

2.08 : Children contributing to the briefing and design process.

Londoners Making London

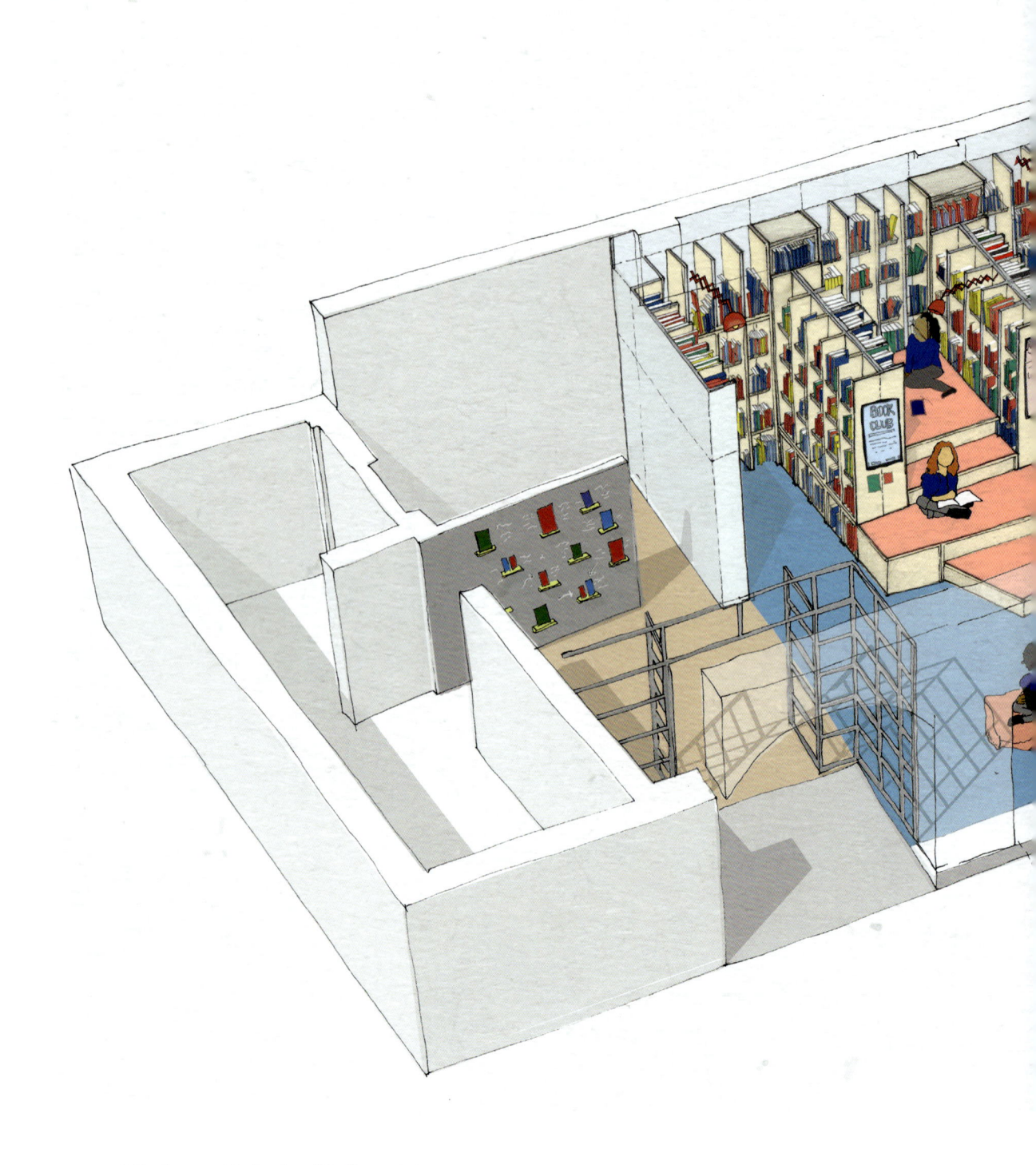

2.09 : Axonometric drawing of the library design. Drawing the design in a manner that could be understood by everyone was essential to keeping the school community engaged.

Chapter 2 | Enterprise + Learning

87

JK   EB + KS

suggesting had a major impact on that. What I know now as a parent-governor is that they had a lot of reasons why they had to be careful and why they had to take it slowly.

You know this very well. Even with the best people in the world, it is a huge challenge in terms of the resources that you need to put into delivering a project like this. Anyone who has ever tried to build anything knows all too well that things are never straightforward and there are always issues and complications. Ultimately, the space we ended up with is everything we had dreamed. It is exciting. It is very different from their classrooms. I love that about it. It's full of wonderful nooks and crannies that encourage children to do what they love to do, which is to find little hidey holes and explore the space in their own way.

One other very important part of the fundraising plan was not only to get this amazing space and to fill it with books, but also to fund a librarian, to try to ensure that the school had ongoing support with this new resource. We have a part-time librarian for three days a week that is funded by one very generous Foundation donor. Now when I go in as a parent governor and I'm doing link visits to observe the library and the English programme in the school, I can see how that is helping support and enhance what the teachers are trying to do. The librarian makes it inspiring. There is a myriad of ways that she's bringing the library to life and helping ensure that it is what we all, parents and school, had hoped it would be.

Emily: Look, there are always going to be people who have different opinions or want different things. Even though the

2.10 : Run Thornhill Run participants at Highbury Fields. The library project was the pretext for the mobilisation of local people which soon extended beyond the school community.
2.11 : Participants warming up for the run.

Chapter 2 | Enterprise + Learning

JK   EB + KS

library was almost a no-brainer, people come to the table with different views and so there wasn't unanimous support for it. There were some concerns around the cost and whether there weren't other things that the money should be spent on. If you are dealing with lots of different people, there are lots of different objectives. But I think once you establish with the senior leadership team that this is something that the children need, then you've just got to really focus on the end goal. You need to try and bring people with you and explain what it's all about and say, yes, it is expensive, but this is why it's worth it and this is why it's an investment and it is not at the cost of other things. We will do those other things too. But there was resistance there and I think I found that challenging. It's a library and I knew it was an amazing thing and I couldn't understand why there were naysayers. But you'll meet them in life, you meet them on every project. It's about spending time with those people to understand their perspective, make sure they're heard, incorporate them in the project, bring them along, as much as you can bring them with you. So these two learnings were a humbling experience, and the lesson is, it's got to be led by the school. It can't be me as a nosy parent saying, 'I want that library for my children.' It's got to be what works for the school and the children.

Jan: What would your advice be to others who have the ambition to realise a project like yours in their community?

Kate: The point is, it's not one person and it's not one thing. It's many people and a collection of things and little things that add up. Inspiring things happen when you create

2.12 : Thornhill pupils helping to raise funding for the library by selling lemonade on their doorstep.

89

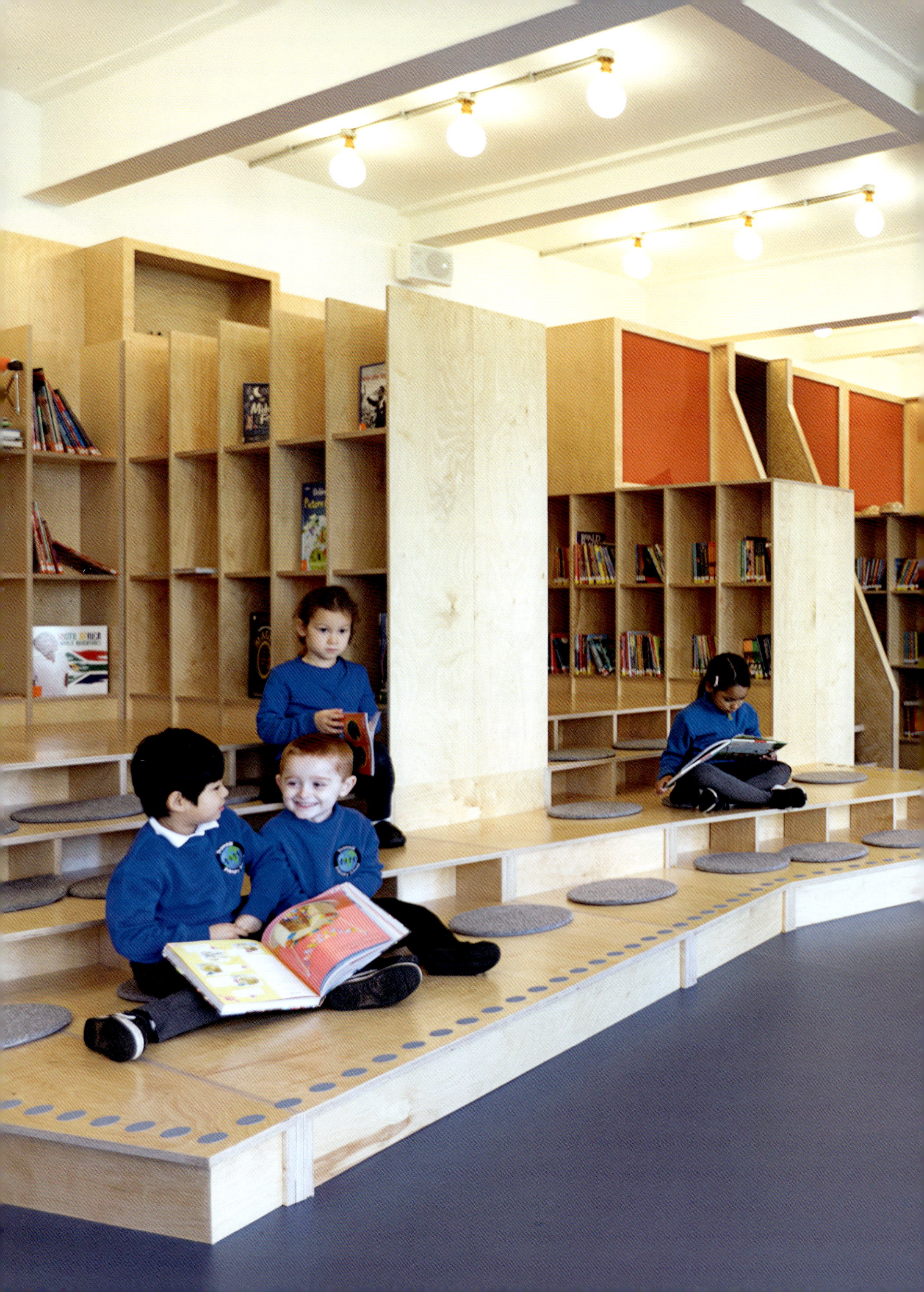

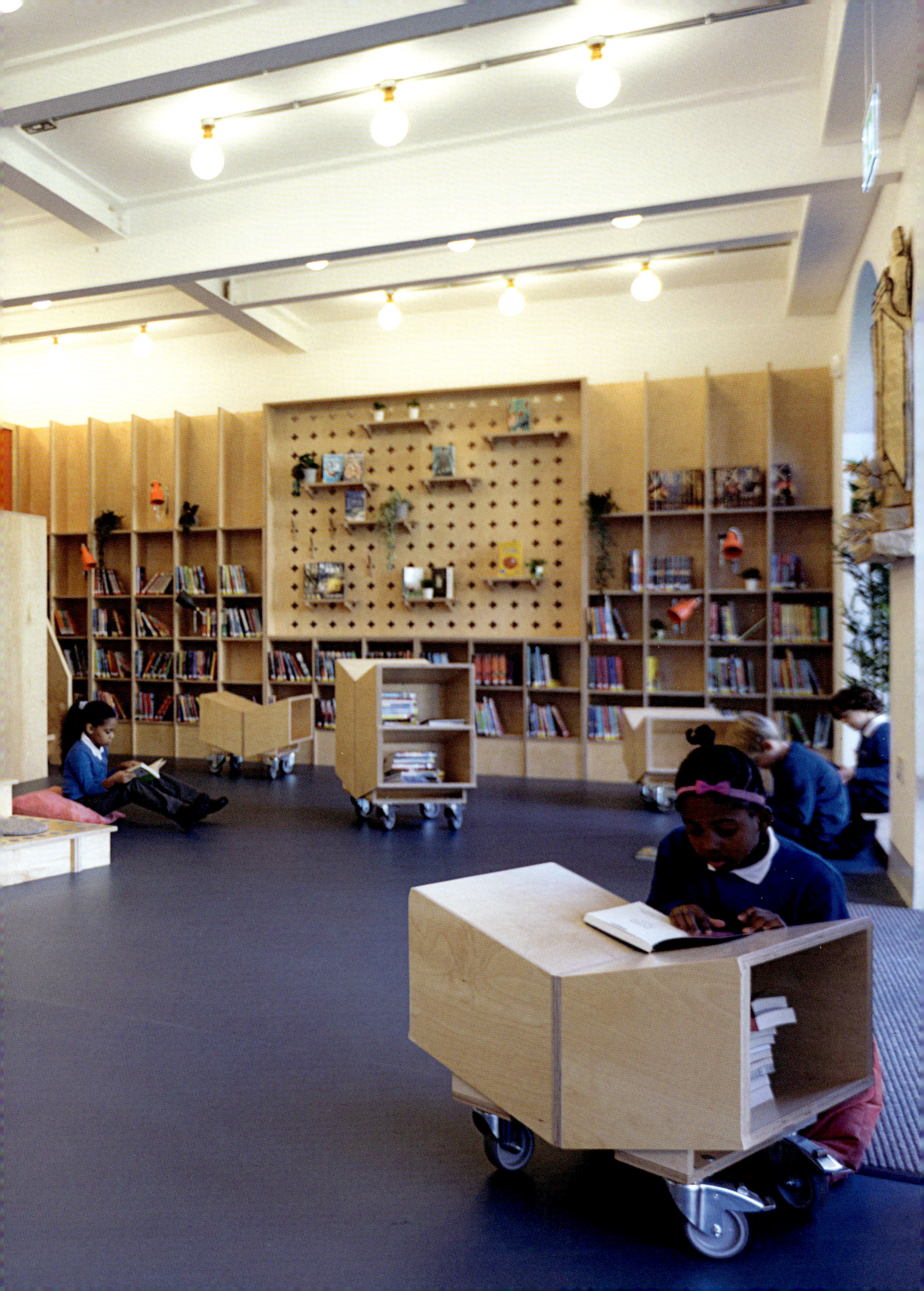

JK   EB + KS

an environment where people feel welcome at the table.

Emily: That's absolutely it. A school is a great place to start because you've already got a community. People already have a bond. Our children are at the school, we want our children to do well, but we also want the best for our neighbours. Good schools make good communities.

Jan: Thank you, Kate and Emily.

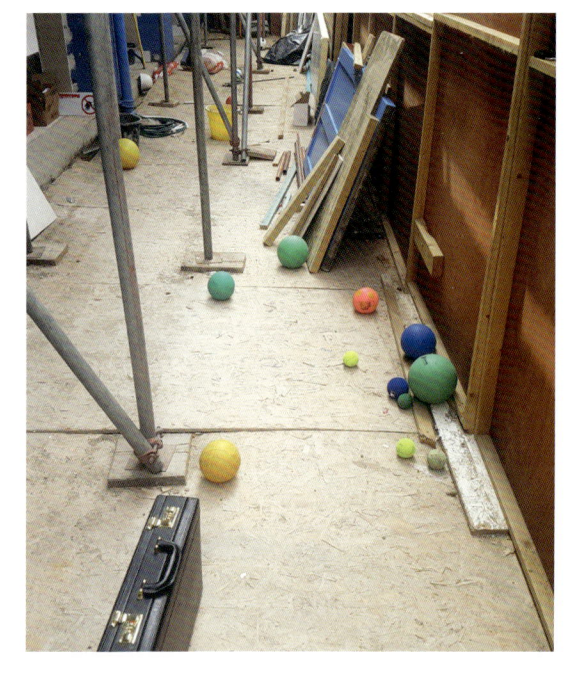

2.13 : [Previous Page] - Thornhill Library interior after completion. Putting an operational plan in place and setting aside funding for a librarian was integral to securing the legacy of the new library.

2.14 : Balls behind the construction hoarding.
2.15 : [ibid]

The Tailoring Academy w/ Jenny Holloway

2019 – Present

London, Harringay Warehouse District, N4

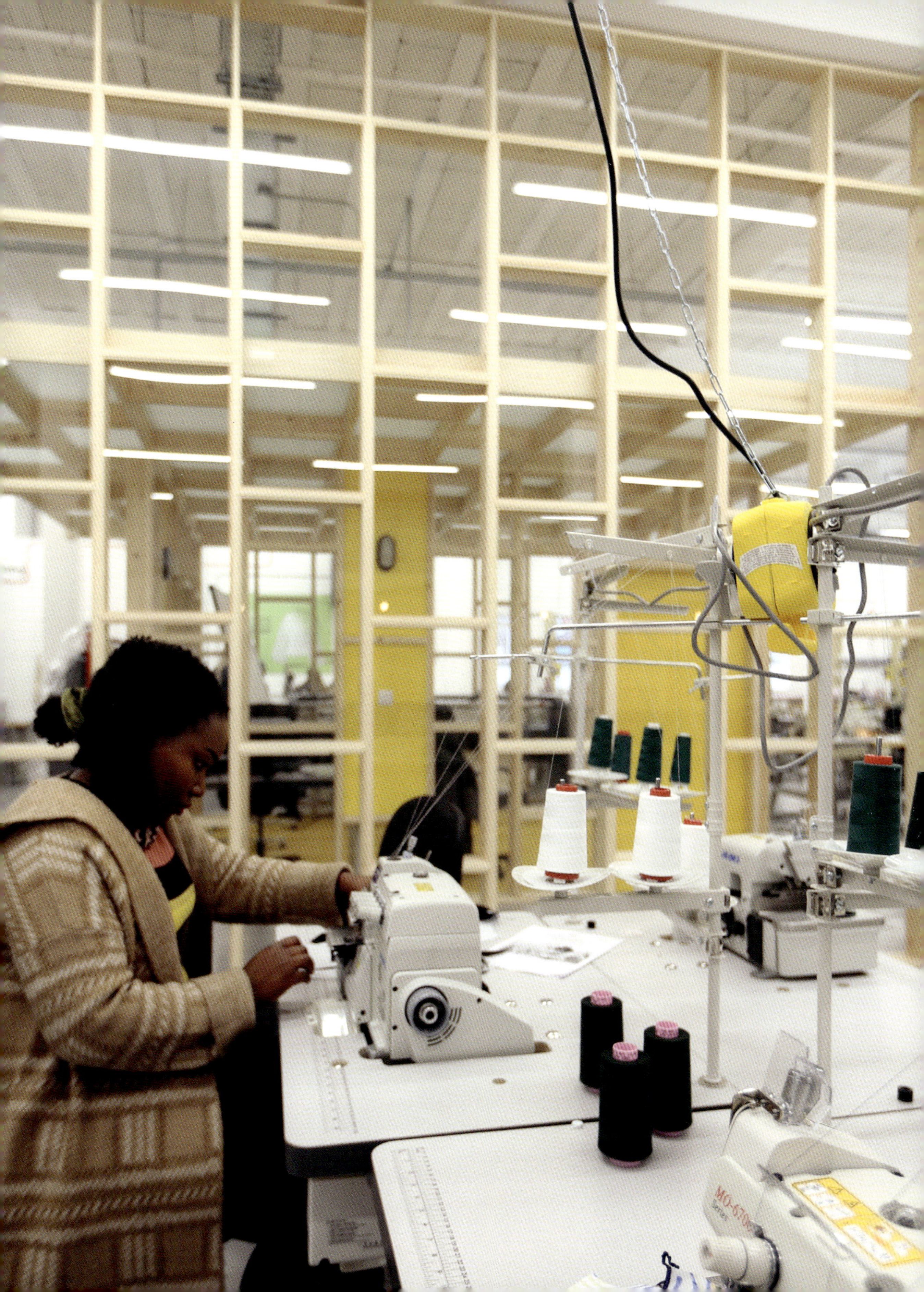

About

Jenny Holloway incorporated Fashion Enter Ltd in 2006 as a not-for-profit social enterprise. Today, it has two aims: to provide outstanding British-made quality garment production and to be a centre of excellence for training and development for technical skills in fashion. There are over 200 employees at Fashion Enter across four locations in Haringey, Islington, Leicester and Wales, and the company produces up to 30,000 quality garments a week from two factories in London and Newtown, Wales. Clients include ASOS, N Brown, Very Group and Community Clothing.

As the business became more and more successful, Jenny realised that there was an urgent demand for a quality training programme in garment manufacturing, and she set up an apprenticeship programme at her factory. In 2015 the training programme expanded to become the UK's first Fashion Technology Academy offering eight new qualifications on the garment life cycle.

In 2019 Fashion Enter launched the Tailoring Academy, a space for both learning and industrial production, bringing fine garment manufacture back to London and tailoring skills to Londoners. The Tailoring Academy is a state-of-the-art clothing manufacturing and training facility which provides specialist skills, job training and apprenticeships in ready-to-wear and bespoke tailoring.

2.16 : [previous page] - The design for the Tailoring Academy creates interdependencies between learning space and manufacturing space.

Chapter 2 | Enterprise + Learning

JK   JH   JK   JH

2.17 : Jenny Holloway, CEO of Fashion Enter.

Jan: Hello Jenny, thank you for making the time to see me. I am intrigued about your motivations in 2006 when you set up Fashion Enter. Garment manufacturing in the UK had been in steady decline since 1926 as companies found cheaper places to manufacture overseas. Eighty years later, hardly any manufacturing remained here, and you decided to reverse the trend. That's quite radical. Why did you do it?

Jenny: I don't agree that there was a major decline from 1926 all the way through until now. I was a selector at Marks & Spencer in the 1970s and 80s. I was there when 94 per cent of everything they sold was made in the UK. I was therefore in a very privileged position to witness the best of quality garment manufacturing at its peak in the 80s and 90s. I visited amazing factories like Burnham in Nottingham. There were rows of machinists who were totally skilled at their jobs, and they were proud of their skills. So proud that they would encourage their children to apply for the same jobs. Today we have garment manufacturing portrayed with the image of the sweatshops and that's so unfair. Being a stitcher is a highly regarded craft and needs to be recognised as a real skill.

I now look back and realise that this period during the 70s and 80s was the golden age of manufacturing. Thousands and thousands of garments were made. An order with Marks & Spencer was raised in 'dozens'. When I was a selector for formal blouses we had an ultramarine blouse and we would order 3000 dozen of a colourway! That is an absolutely phenomenal quantity, allowing for a factory to invest in the future, train and forward plan with confidence. I don't believe those days will ever come back, as there is now so much choice in the marketplace, with instant gratification on delivery. But with a new emphasis on ethical and sustainable clothing, I still think there's a major place for 'made in the UK'. Now more than ever, we need compliant and audited factories that can provide proximity sourcing and one-piece flow so we stop overproduction going to landfill and reduce carbon emissions.

At the moment, retailers are chasing prices to the bottom, running around the globe trying to shave off 50 cents. It's criminal. Price has to be the lowest common denominator, yet that is the intake margin. What about the exit margin! That's what counts. There is no point ordering 5000 garments to shave off 20 pence on a garment to then discount 33 per cent of the order because it has not sold. Surely it's more cost effective to spend a little more but reduce the quantity right down, contribute to the UK economy and reduce emissions. I don't get it!

I've always loved manufacturing and I wanted to reverse that trend, but it wasn't

97

JK   JH

'let's open a factory.' It didn't happen like that. The company started in 2006 and we had £8k worth of share money that I had. That's all I had, and I invested in a shop in Croydon. It was a very gradual transfer from retail to manufacturing.

Jan: Amazing. What were the challenges along the way? You've grown very organically. There must've been bumps?

Jenny: Oh, yes …! Not so much bumps as huge mountains! We were helping lots of designers and then we would recommend a designer to a CMT. That's a Cut, Make and Trim unit. And then they would ring me up on a Saturday in floods of tears, saying 'you recommended this person, they've let me down, they've overcharged me, their samples are rubbish.' So, I opened a small sampling unit. That's how we started with manufacturing.

The biggest single challenge was my personal lack of knowledge. It's one skill to create samples for designers, but it's totally a different skill to efficiently run a factory.

I had a very fortuitous conversation with Nick Robertson and Nick Beighton of ASOS in around 2010. Nick Robertson was the CEO, and Nick Beighton was a CFO. We met at a press launch for which we'd made some samples. I made a passing comment to Nick Beighton and said, you're going to need a factory one day. If you want to do fast-track fashion, you have to look at the UK. Nick Robertson said, 'Oh, that's a great idea. How much do you think that's going to cost?' I thought, this is a golden opportunity, I'm not going to let this one go. I didn't have a clue how much it was going to cost but said it would be around £250k. Six weeks

JK   JH

later, £238k landed in our account, and we started a factory.

Jan: Was that the moment when you moved from Croydon to Harringay?

Jenny: No, we'd moved to Harringay already earlier, with the sampling unit. We called it The Workshop to start off with. I always knew what I wanted The Workshop and factory to be – I learned this from my retail trade and knew the importance of ethics, compliance and true diversity within the workplace. However, knowing what you want, and implementing are two very different matters. Everyone can have a file of policies, strategies and objectives, but it's the processes of implementing them in a way that makes every part of the factory lean, efficient and measurable. I also wasn't happy with a standard factory, I wanted Fashion Enter to be outstanding in all respects. To achieve that requires huge effort and a great team that has a similar mindset.

Similar to meeting the two Nicks from ASOS, in business you need to network and meet the right people. Fortunately for me, I had met a wonderful man called Michael Chambini who was the manager of the Florentia Clothing Village. We were outgrowing our workspace and we needed a new factory premises, and Michael supported that growth. He also networked me with some fantastic stitchers who are still employed by us today. Moving to larger premises gave us the space to really expand and grow.

Ultimately, the Florentia site proved to be problematic. There were factories employing illegal immigrants. One day we

Chapter 2 | Enterprise + Learning

JK   JH

witnessed a Home Office raid and I saw people hanging out the windows trying to escape, as they didn't have UK eligibility. I knew then that I couldn't stay at the site. I then found Crusader Estate, and we were supporting Remploy who were in Unit 14. There had been a change in government policy, and they were closing down the Remploy factories and I knew the unit would come up for rent. I had worked with Remploy employees for about 12 months, and I was keen to keep some of them employed. Today, I still have two ex-Remploy people, and they make a very valuable contribution to the company.

Moving from Florentia to Crusader was a huge jump in space and rent. The rent was three times the rent we were paying at Florentia, so it was a huge decision. I remember taking the dog for a walk for something like three hours as I kept analysing and reviewing if the risk was too great. At the end I thought, you know what, sometimes you have to make a decision and then make that decision work. There is not a right or wrong decision, it's about commitment, dedication and hard work! So, we moved! It was awful to start off with because the bills were just so high. We didn't know how to organise a huge factory correctly and our expertise was still quite raw. As a CEO, you have to take that responsibility and you need to lead by example. I learned really quickly and read a lot.

Jan: And then you expanded here? And since then, you have acquired factories in Wales?

Jenny: Yes. Timing is everything in business, and we have literally 'popped' in size over

2.18 : Open day at the Tailoring Academy. Engaging new audiences and raising the profile of garment manufacture is an important part of Fashion Enter's mission.

99

Londoners Making London

2.19 : Glazed wooden screen separating learning and manufacturing spaces. Creating a nurturing environment is integral to shifting the common perception of manufacturing.

Chapter 2 | Enterprise + Learning

JK JH

the last few years. I am very proud of the factory today; we have brought in new systems of performance-related pay and new audits, worked with our staff and created an amazing factory and team. We are the only factory in the UK that has a leading status in the ethical Fast Forward Audit, and we are SMETA (Sedex Members Ethical Trade Audit) audited too. We have no 'non-compliances', which is an amazing achievement.

People may sometimes look at the role of a CEO and just not realise how much work goes on in the background. You have to lead by example and no job is too small and none too large. There were times early on when finances were so tight that you had to micro-manage the cashflow; times when you have to roll up your sleeves and get the orders out on time and other times when you are guest speaker at a conference providing insights into the future. It's a challenging and diverse role, but only possible with a great team behind you!

Manufacturing is only one area of the business. We have other hats such as education; we are landlord of an incubation space; we have a retail shop now; and we have also led a European Social Fund programme.

My passion really lies in education. We operate very much like a community centre! People come on our courses and don't want to leave. They're here two weeks, a month or six months and longer. I'd rather we operate like this, in an inclusive way, knowing that we've given hope to somebody, rather than ticking a box and saying, 'Right. You've passed. Here's your certificate, off you go!'

JK JH

Jan: You're not only manufacturing in the UK. You're also educating a whole new generation of fashion entrepreneurs with skills that industry previously had outsourced to other parts of the world. How did you manage to revive garment manufacturing as an appealing career for young people?

Jenny: Well, that's still ongoing. I would say that we've made significant progress on the image of the industry, with many short videos on Fashion Capital, our YouTube channel, but this is ongoing and there is still work to be undertaken.

One of the major advancements we have made for the industry is creating a new system of performance-related pay with Galaxius. Machinists use phones to scan in their barcode, so we know exactly who has made what and when and how much they are paid. This is true transparency and helps support our ethical trading objectives. It took us four years to develop Galaxius with a great guy, Mark Randle, and this system is now really recognised as a benchmark of excellence. Our machinists here are paid anywhere between £11 and £19 an hour, due to the way the operations are set up – true performance-related pay.

Jan: Tell me a little bit about the academy and the educational programme that you run. What's really interesting, and I think quite unusual, about your business, is that you're training the people that ultimately will work for you and in that way you invest in both the business but also the people.

Jenny: Before Brexit, we realised that there were just not enough British stitchers. We placed adverts in local papers and

101

Londoners Making London

JK   JH

on the radio and more and more people would approach us from Eastern European countries. Prior to Brexit it was a daily occurrence for people to knock on the door and ask for a job. There was just no issue of skills shortages. However, with Brexit and the run-up to Brexit, many of our stitchers were hurt and offended. They left and didn't return, and now the door does not buzz anymore with skilled Eastern Europeans requesting a job. Hence the need for the Stitching Academy.

ASOS gave us £72k to buy machines for the Stitching Academy, and I reviewed the current qualifications that were available for stitching. I was appalled! There were many different awarding bodies, but none had qualifications for stitching! So, I decided to write a qualification alongside the UK Fashion and Textile Association and an amazing man, John West. At least that way I knew it was industry-ready and to the requirements of a factory. We created two courses, level one and two for both stitching and pattern-making. The stitching level one is one of the most popular qualifications with awarding body Skills and Education Group, and it's particularly strong in Scotland. That makes me feel as though we've helped the whole of the nation. It has been incredibly successful, not just for people becoming our production machinists, but for those designers that want to open up their own collections. It is much easier for them to make the garment and save money to start off with, rather than ordering 5000 garments from China.

Jan: There is also an element of lifelong mentoring that you as an organisation and you personally take very seriously. I suppose the workspace and the pop-up shop you're

2.20 : View towards new entrance door.

Chapter 2 | Enterprise + Learning

2.21 : New foyer for the Tailoring Academy. An open and welcoming foyer gives the building a public face on the street.

Londoners Making London

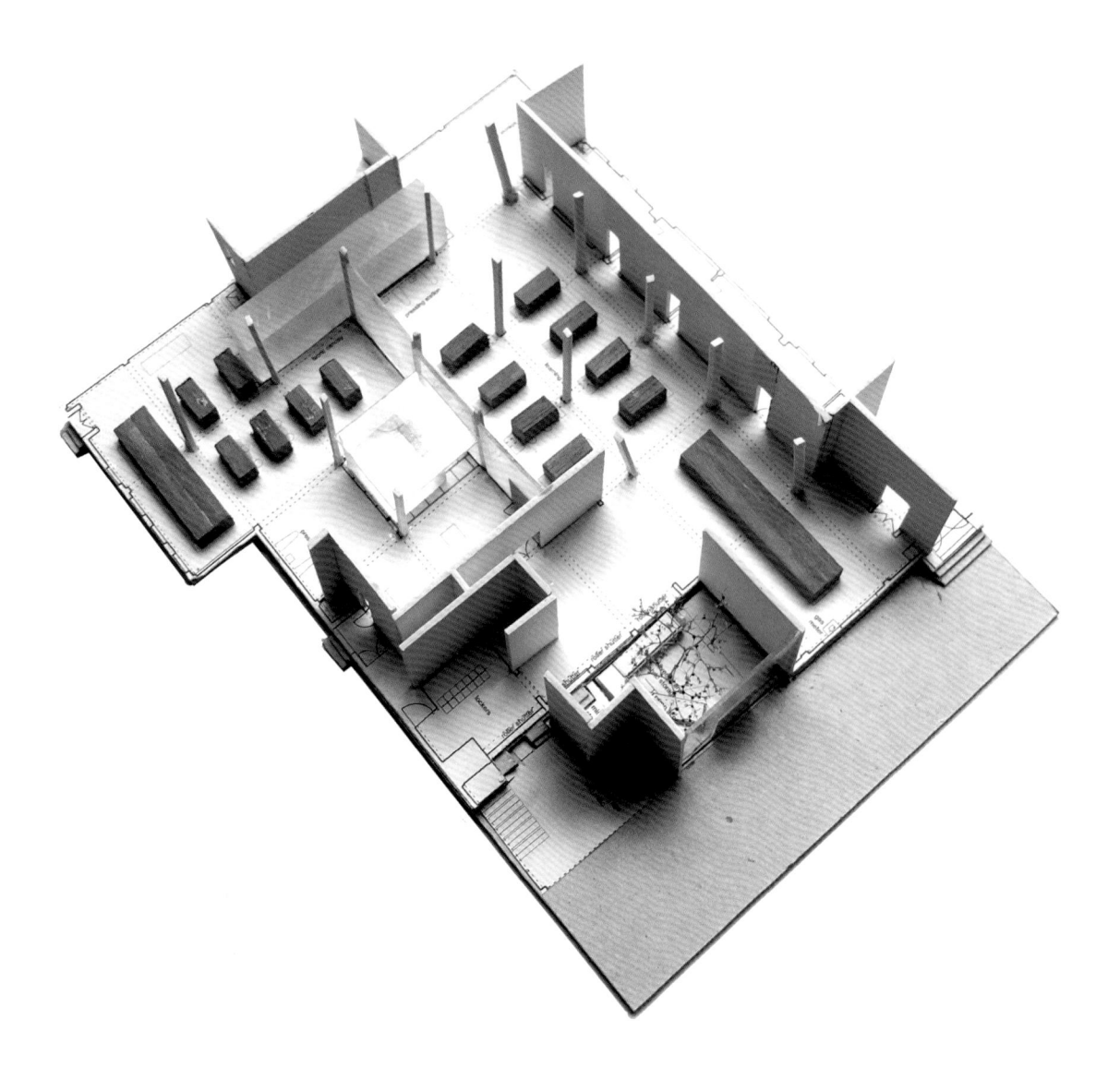

2.22 : Concept model of the design strategy.
Physical models are a more inclusive way of
engaging with people outside the built environment.

JK   JH

running in Finsbury Park are part of that commitment? It'd be great to hear a little bit about that, being trained by you here and then benefiting from lifelong support and mentoring. Is that the future of education?

> Jenny: It's the most rewarding part of the job to have a business that creates social good, and this can be measured through the Social Value Matrix. We have a diverse number of programmes on at the moment, and it's stimulating to keep organically growing into new parts of the social side. In Leicester we won the Community Renewal Fund, helping businesses and individuals to upskill. We also have an affordable workspace programme which is a £10m project through the Greater London Authority's Good Growth Fund over ten years. However, this is a capital spend, so we are not funded to run that programme. It is an amazing programme. It incorporates a complete circular economy project within Islington, whereby there is incubation space and then a retail shop with mentoring provided. It's the first of its kind as far as I know. How innovative of Islington Council! The shop is based on Fonthill Road, which was absolutely iconic in the 1970s and 80s. However, Fonthill Road, it was built on 'cabbage' – do you know what cabbage is?

Jan: In relation to your industry, I do not.

> Jenny: Cabbage is over-makes of garments. Manufacturing was absolutely thriving in the UK in the 70s when Marks & Spencer, John Lewis, the Arcadia Group made in the UK, and London was a major manufacturing cluster. There would be over-makes and runners would buy up the leftovers, the cabbage, and sell it on to the markets and wholesalers. There were absolute bargains

JK   JH

of course, as the garments would be a fraction of the retail price. Those days have long gone now.

The Fonthill Road project is brilliant, reaching a really wide cross-section of people. It's one of the best projects I have worked on, and in September 2022 we created £106k of social value.

In Wales I have just started a great social project. I have a friend, Jean Balmer, who I have known since I was 18. She's a shepherdess. I went to see her a few years ago and she had piles of fleeces stacked up rotting. I said, 'What a waste, why aren't you using that wool?' She said 'They are not worth anything. Nobody wants to buy them; it costs me £1.50 to remove the fleece and I am paid 90p for the fleece itself.' So I contacted the Welsh government and I said, this is actually ridiculous. Wool is a beautiful fibre you must be able to do something with it. This resulted in us being awarded a very small budget for a feasibility study to take place to combine Welsh wool fibres with a recycled fibre to generate a new type of yarn that could be used. We worked with the Potter Group for this programme: they are waste specialists in Welshpool. We are now hoping for further funding to take this approach to produce woven fabrics.

Jan: So technology and skills are important?

> Jenny: Well, I'm really glad you said that. There's now such a chronic shortage of really skilled machinists that can get up and go, that you have to look at alternatives. Printing is a dirty part of textiles production. It pollutes rivers and landscapes. The alternatives are state-of-the-art printing machines and cutting machines.

2.23 : [next page] - Foyer of The Tailoring Academy.

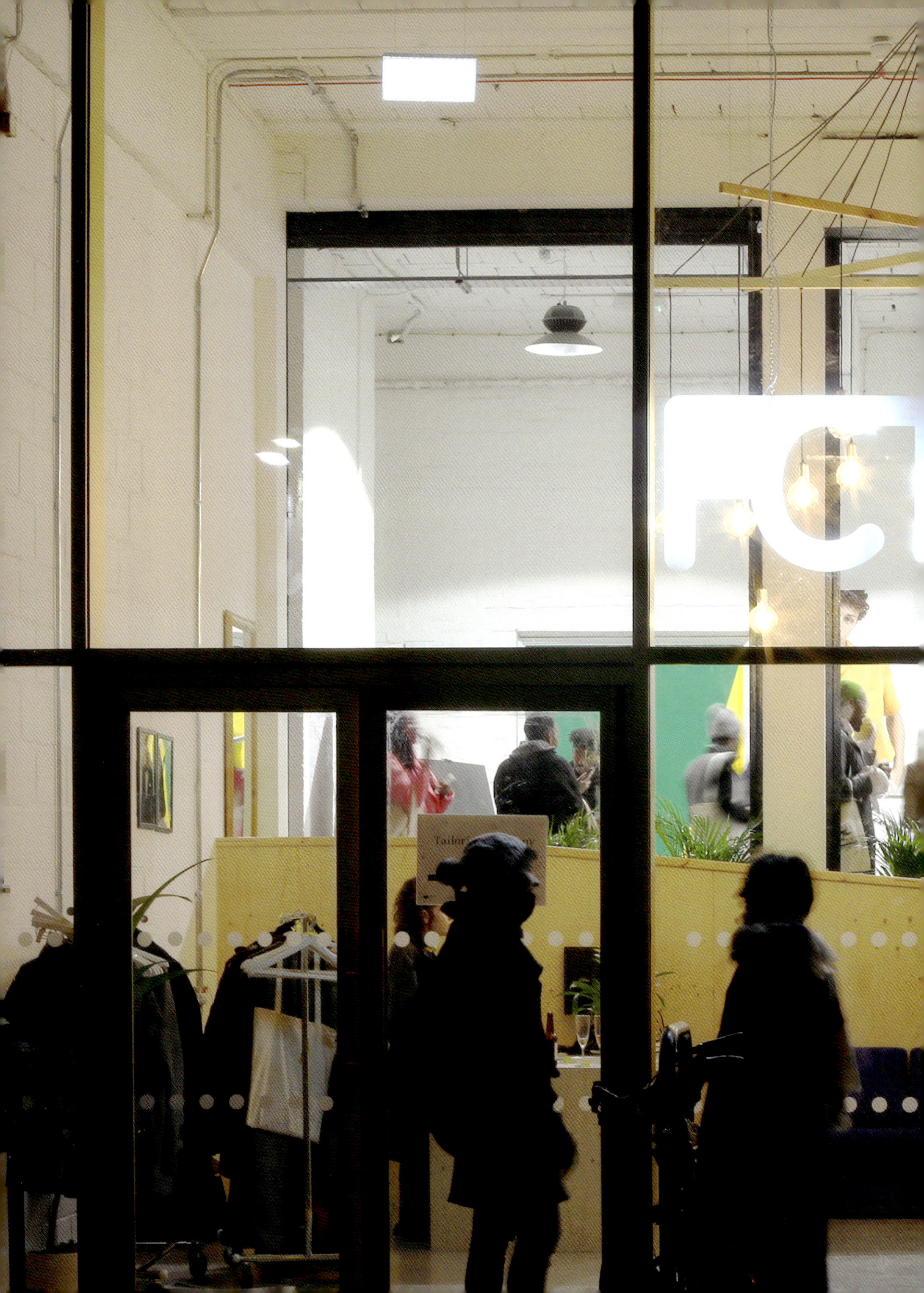

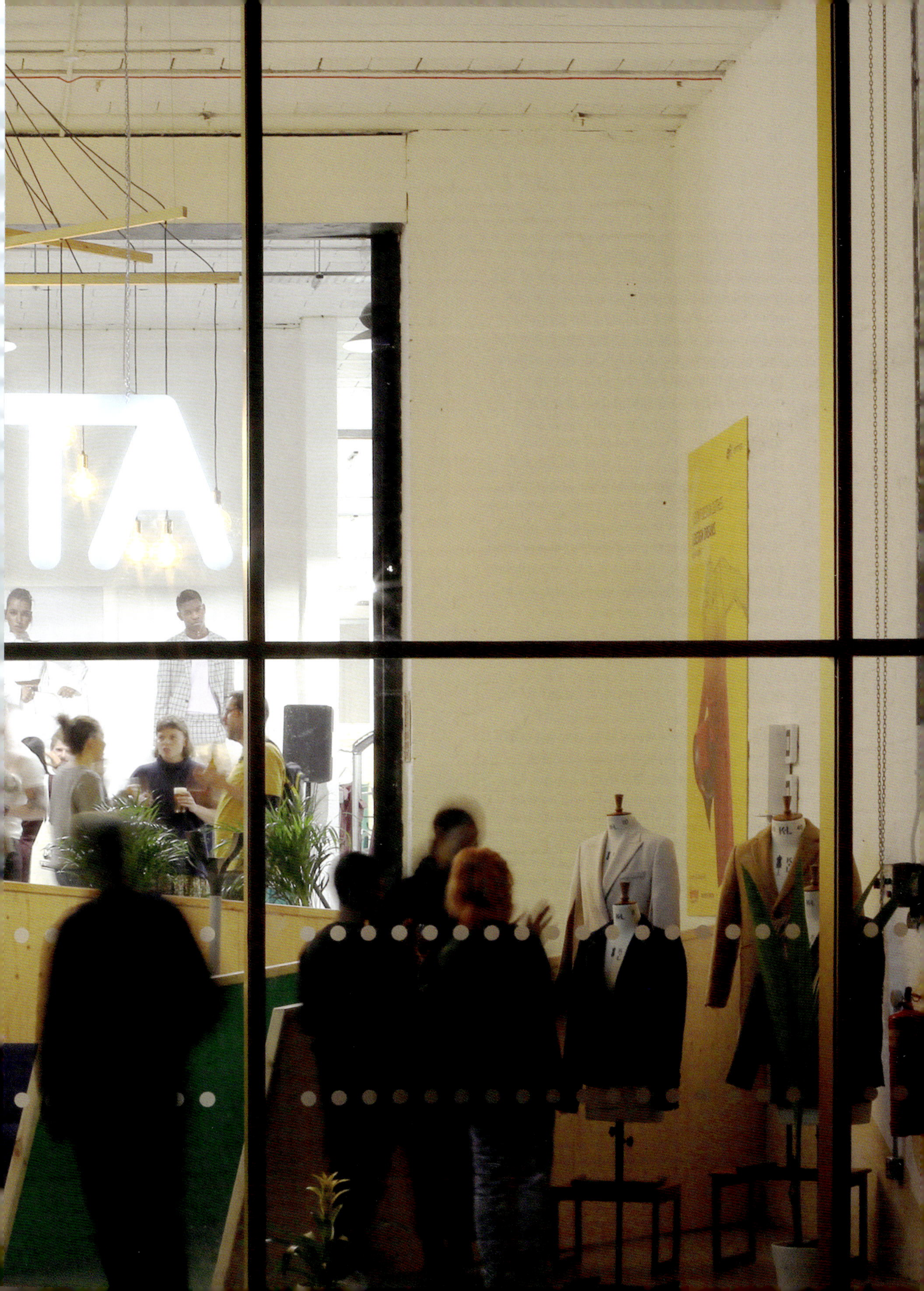

Londoners Making London

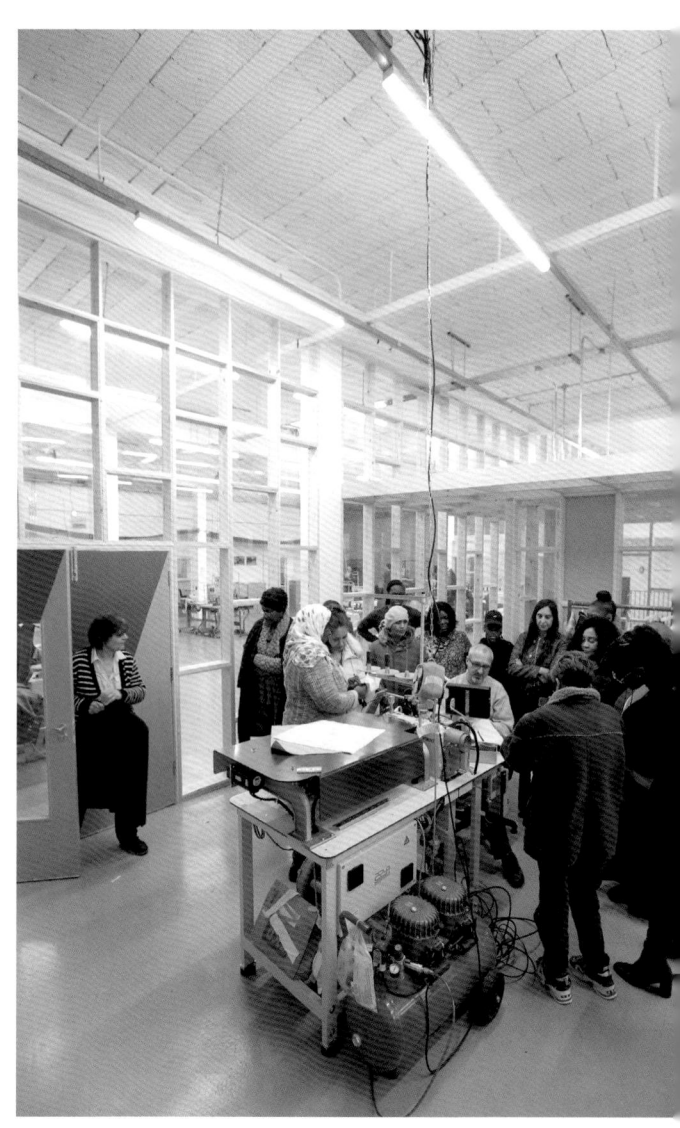

110

Chapter 2 | Enterprise + Learning

2.27 : 2.31 : Contemporary garment design and manufacture combines analogue and digital technologies, reducing waste and making small, local production runs an economically viable possibility.

111

Church Grove w/ Anurag Verma + Jon Broome

2018 – Present

London, Lewisham, SE13

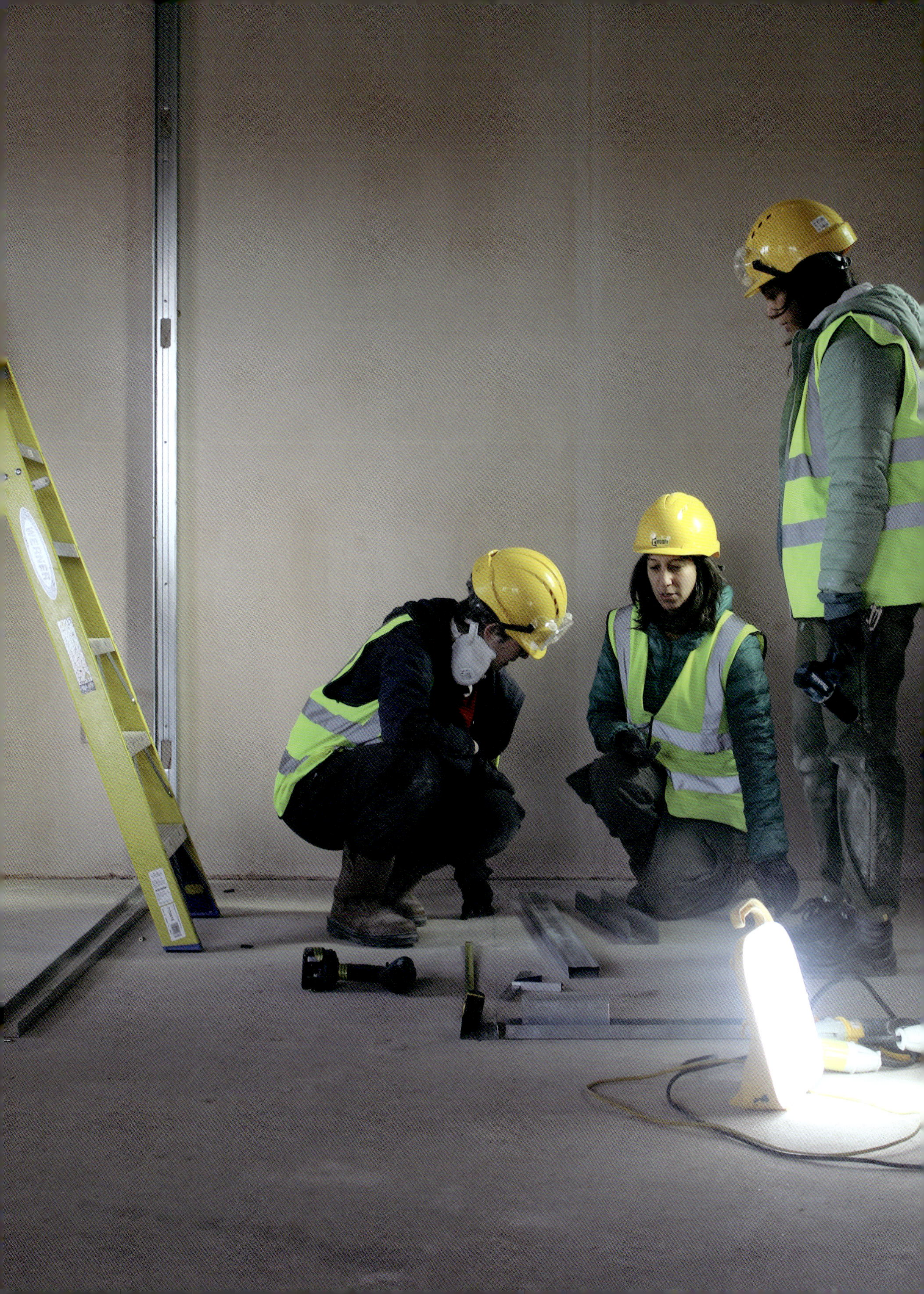
WERNER

About

The Rural Urban Synthesis Society (RUSS) was set up in 2009 in response to both the housing crisis and climate change. The name is a reflection on the fact that 2008 was the year that for the first time more than 50 per cent of the world's population lived in cities as opposed to subsistence rural living. And for a city like London to become 'sustainable' ultimately will require us to become reconnected with how our food and energy are produced and consumed.

The organisation now has 1100 members. It is formally constituted as a Community Land Trust and registered as a Community Benefit Society with charitable status.

Church Grove in Lewisham is RUSS's first community-led housing project. Once completed, the development will provide 36 residential units of varying size and tenure along with communal spaces such as laundry, guest room and offices. Future residents have been involved in the design process, and many of them have opted to contribute to the construction as self-builders.

Building on the legacy of architect Walter Segal, who led the delivery of two previous community-built housing projects in Lewisham, in Walters Way and Segal Close during the 1980s, RUSS wants to establish community-led housing as a viable and accessible way of building homes. The RUSS School now shares its experiences and lessons learned during the conception, design and construction of Church Grove.

Anurag Verma is Chair of RUSS. He presents a series of modules sharing RUSS's knowledge of its development journey at the RUSS School and assesses the development potential of future sites. As a National Community Land Trust Network ambassador, he promotes the benefits of sustainable self-build development. Committed to education and design, he previously taught architectural history and is currently engaged in architectural practice.

Jon Broome is an architect with a particular interest in environmental design. He grew up in Church Grove and has been involved in RUSS since its inception, initially on a voluntary basis, then as a consultant and more recently as a volunteer member of the Church Grove project board where he is acting as design advisor.

2.32 : [previous page] Self-builders at Church Grove.

JK   AV + JB   JK   AV + JB

Jan: Thank you very much for taking the time to speak to me. Can we start with introductions? Church Grove is a big project that has been running for several years and many people are involved. What has your role been?

Anurag: I have been involved in RUSS since 2018, both as Chair and as a volunteer. As the latter, Jon and I look into future sites and future projects. I also manage the RUSS School where we call guests to talk to groups of people who are interested in our community. We talk them through the various phases of community-led housing. RUSS has a very particular way of teaching, which is completely based on our experience. There are five stages to setting up a community-led housing group. The modules we offer now are: group, site, plan and we are developing the build module. Once everybody has moved in, we will offer the fifth module, called 'live'. The first module is about developing constitutional objectives and setting up your governance structure. During the second stage you look for a site. The third stage culminates with securing planning permission and then getting a tender out. The fourth stage is the build.

RUSS wants to share this experience from the long journey that we have embarked on, which nobody thought would take as long.

Jon: I am an architect. My link to RUSS is through Kareem Dayes. Kareem is the son of one of the original self-builders from the Walters Way community in Lewisham. His dad built their family house in the 80s and he had the privilege to grow up at Walters Way, so by default he knew about self-building.

It was 'normal' to him that people built their own homes. Then as a student he moved into Sanford Housing Co-op and discovered all about housing co-operatives. But most importantly, he and his brothers helped their dad to retrofit the family home, which involved installing a ground-source heat pump, underfloor heating, photovoltaics, triple-glazed windows and reinsulating the home.

This rebuild project introduced Kareem to the concept of micro-generation and really inspired him. It made him ask the question, 'Why can't there be more homes like this?' He couldn't afford to live in London and began to explore the idea of a new self-build project but with sustainability through energy production and food production incorporated within it. This was the vision for RUSS.

Kareem came around my place one afternoon. We sat down on the lawn, and we talked about his vision. Kareem is very idealistic. I saw my role as being the one to turn his vision into something that could be built and that somebody would put money into.

2.33 : Jon Broome, RUSS associate and Anurag Verma, Chair of RUSS.

JK   AV + JB

There was a small community of half a dozen people sitting around the kitchen table, asking themselves 'what are we?', 'what are we going to do?' and 'how are we going to fund it?' And things progressed from here. It took shape in my mind as creating a sustainable neighbourhood in the city. This meshed with what Kareem was interested in, in terms of energy, sustainable living and growing in the city.

Kareem used part of his student loan to set up a record label with his brothers and bandmates, releasing their own records and hosting music events around London. Each flyer and record said, 'All profits go towards creating a sustainable community.' They managed to fundraise about £6k, which was enough to create RUSS as a Community Benefit Society and get the ball rolling. This was followed by a non-profit community share issue where we raised about £20k and grew the membership to about 250. It was at around this time that we first approached Lewisham and the Greater London Authority.

Lewisham had promoted Walter Segal's self-built schemes originally. In the 90s I was involved in building about ten co-operative self-built projects in Lewisham. But, astonishingly, Council officers had never heard of this work. There was nobody in the local authority who had any idea. When I left college, I worked for Lewisham for a little while. There were 300 people in the architects' department at the time. There's not one architect employed by the Council now.

I then wrote a paper which explained what had happened in the past. I knew about the Church Grove site, because I grew up next

JK   AV + JB

door. We worked up a business plan based on the site. It was difficult because the Council had tried to develop the site before, but Church Grove residents had resisted. My grandmother lived in Church Grove and my brother lived in Church Grove, and they fought the proposals and won. After that, it was always going to be an issue to get permission for something that aligned with Kareem's vision and that the locals would go along with. Many of them did in the end, and some of them are members of RUSS now. But some of them are opposed to the development. They had an alternative idea about a community garden on the site. But the Council rejected the idea.

After we shared the paper, the Council perked up and said, 'Well that's all very interesting, but I think we could do it better.' And they went on to commission a feasibility study and called a public meeting. They said, 'We want to do something self-build, is anyone interested?' And a lot of local people came along and said 'yes'. Then nothing happened for about a year and a half. So we went back to the Council and said, 'You know, we've actually got a proposal for the site.' They said, 'Let's have another look at it,' and we ended up speaking to someone in the housing strategy team. The Council's advice was that we would have to provide a justification to dispose of the site for a nominal amount.

We went through the entire argument and got academics to support us. There is an established way of measuring social value. But that did not wash with the solicitor, who said, 'It's got to go into a competition.' They were asking us to compete against developers, basically. We then mounted a legal case, based on three legal opinions.

JK　　AV + JB

The case said it was not necessary to compete and that competition was a waste of time and money. We had top housing lawyers. Nevertheless, we did not make progress.

So a whole competitive tender process was instigated. We did manage to argue, however, that the criteria should be favourable to creating social value. It was not a straight competition, but a competitive dialogue. Broadly speaking, it had several stages you had to go through. It took a year and cost us a lot of money. You basically have to design the entire project in detail and present evidence on how you would finance it. We had to get banks behind it. We had to get opinions from the planning authority and provide a whole lot of detail.

Anurag: I think that's a good point. RUSS has got to where it is through learning by doing. Every challenge that we encountered prompted us to develop our organisation's capacity. Going through the competitive tender process meant that we had a

JK　　AV + JB

strategy, we had a business plan, we had a project manager, we had to formalise our aims and objectives, and we had a pretty good idea what the project was going to cost.

Every time we've had to go and ask for money from a public body, we have had to make a good value argument. They make you jump through a lot of hoops. I think it cuts both ways though. One of the reasons why we are here today is that RUSS has always had great input from really qualified people who are passionate and dedicated to helping us. To deliver housing requires you to be accountable to multiple stakeholders. Going through all these steps has helped us to understand the procurement system. None of us has been through housing development as a process.

Jon: I had obviously been involved in designing housing, but not developing housing. The work we did all had to be done anyway. In our case it came framed in a way that made it unnecessarily onerous though.

Jan: I suppose you were following an established process, but you had very different parameters. So the two, process and objectives, didn't fit together any more.

Anurag: Yes. I think this is what we've learned. What I've learned is that this is about a lot of people working together. We wouldn't be here without Council support, without support from the Greater London Authority, without our funders' support, without our members' support and the commitment of our volunteers.

There is one thing that is quite unique to the way we work. There are quite a few

2.34 : RUSS members signing the development agreement at the town hall in 2016.

Chapter 2 | Enterprise + Learning

117

JK   AV + JB

Community Land Trusts who get planning permission but then give the development over to a housing association. What RUSS is doing is delivering the project with our core volunteers overseeing it and putting hours and hours of time into it. Volunteers are co-delivering the project with professionals.

We are builders, we are developers, we are a land trust, and we are a community. I am always amazed how ambitious that vision is.

Jon: I think it's been absolutely critical that RUSS has maintained its independence through the process. If there have been allowances that had to be made, and adjustments, that happened in the face of organisations that don't share the same approach. When RUSS has been in control, we've managed to get what we wanted. When you look at it, we are a bunch of people off the street and the banks have come up and said, here's £11m to deliver your project. This is a big ask. But they've been happy to do that because they've seen that the organisation is competent.

Also, it's been really important in the meetings with the Council that we were able to say, 'We've got a thousand members.' This gives substance to the organisation.

Jan: How is RUSS governed? And how do you organise such a big organisation?

Anurag: It's quite straightforward. We have an elected board of trustees. The tenure for board members is initially three years. You can be re-elected, but the maximum tenure on the board is eight years. We have an annual general meeting where we publish our accounts, update the business strategy and our business plan. The trustees meet

JK   AV + JB

every six weeks, but during this current, critical phase of the build we meet as and when needed. The trustees delegate authority to various sub-committees. The Church Grove sub-committee comprises an executive member from the board plus other volunteer members and the project team. The sub-committee has been delegated a budget and they report back to the main board. We also have a finance and audit sub-committee, and we have a future projects working group and we have the school group, which has a really important role to play. We want to do more projects. And then we have paid staff, an interim managing director and a part-time bookkeeper and admin assistant, and quite a few dedicated volunteers, like Jon. The backbone of RUSS really are the volunteers who have been working tirelessly since the bid for the site, going above and beyond to deliver this. As a client on a construction project, as a developer, there is a lot you have to do. People want to be involved with RUSS, and it's turned out to be really beneficial. People come to us wanting to learn about self-build or wanting to get skills, skills their professional life does not offer them. There have been project managers, quantity surveyors, architects, designers, accountants. It's often touch and go, but I think there is resilience in working like that, resilience that is probably not available in a hierarchical structure.

Jan: Works at Church Grove are progressing at pace. Jon, you spoke about creating a sustainable neighbourhood earlier. How does the building that's now being built live up to this aspiration?

Jon: RUSS was aiming at 100 per cent affordable homes. They had to be as

JK **AV + JB**

affordable as was humanly possible. That included also having low running costs, low energy requirements. The Council had ambitions to involve the community. The idea was that the project wouldn't just be open to people who were going to be housed; instead, it would draw in people from the outside who might want to acquire skills and knowledge. The hub building where we are sitting now was built by volunteers.

The idea was that this sustainable neighbourhood would reflect the general population in this area of London. We needed to provide a range of unit sizes and types, and a varying cost for the dwellings to match the household composition locally and the income profile. We looked at income stats and household stats and created a mix. We included shared flats, one-bedroom flats, flats with below-market rent, two-, three- and four-bedroom dwellings. It was important in our mind to get that kind of spread and to include bigger family dwellings, as they are in short supply.

So we ended up with a mix of shared-ownership flats, fixed-equity sales and social rent. And there's a cross-subsidy involved. If RUSS sells 80 per cent equity in a dwelling, then that can subsidise the social rent of another flat. Balancing all that was a very crucial decision at the beginning. The model that RUSS worked up has taken quite a lot of effort to deliver. Mixing up the various tenures and unit types introduces additional legal and financial complexity.

Anurag: When RUSS started, people were no longer familiar with delivering community-led housing. We were at the forefront of the process. And we were

JK **AV + JB**

ambitious. Although, sometimes, getting people into their homes as quickly as possible is as important as delivering a pure vision. You have to weigh them against each other.

Jan: We have talked about the benefits in terms of affordability and education. But if these benefits could be delivered in other ways, why do community-led housing? Why spend such a long time?

Anurag: Because of the idea of land being held in trust by a community. I think it's absolutely brilliant. I mean, that's what sells it to me. For me personally, the idea that you can commodify land in a market where people spend their time climbing a property ladder is contrary to what a home is. A home is about long-term stability. In particular, when you have 36 families living together, it is really important that the value is in the resource and in the people, the time you spend cultivating friendships, the time you spend living together. The model is committed in the long term to the social, emotional and mental well-being of inhabitants, rather than commercial or financial objectives. I love that.

Jon: That's very big. Kareem grew up in a very successful community. Walters Way is a small group of houses which were built incredibly cheaply by residents. Everybody who has done it will tell you that it was hard work, but it was so worthwhile. And what's of interest to me is that only two of the original self-builders are still there after 40 years, but that for whatever reason the people who have come in have joined because of what the group is about. I'm very strongly of the view that unless people have some stake in the place where they

JK   AV + JB

live, they are missing out. It is clear that it helps people's health. There are so many benefits to having cohesive communities. A precondition for this is that people actually have a say over the decisions that affect their neighbourhood. At RUSS that's at the front of our thinking. Most social housing providers aren't interested in this kind of thing.

Anurag: There is an idea that sustainability has to do with technology. Whereas, in reality, for something to be sustainable it has to have a community and people adopting a way of life. Another thing that's worth mentioning is that in Walters Way, the residents had the right to buy the land. And today you couldn't afford to buy there. One of our central terms of resale is that the value is retained in the site. What that means is that when you buy a property it is affordable. When you leave it, we will resell it at a rate that ensures it is affordable for the next person coming in. You don't walk away with a profit. The dwelling's value is not pegged to the market. We've tried to be really transparent. We said, this is what it's cost to build, and that's what you pay for it. And then, when you leave, we pay a small uplift linked to inflation and we keep the property affordable by selling it to the next person below market value. Other land trusts are adopting a similar model. If you cannot decouple the cost of the home from the market value, it becomes a commodity; its price keeps rising and you lock people out. RUSS also retains a small amount of equity in the homes to keep that resource in the community.

Jon: When we complete this building, councils and banks will look at us completely differently. It's the first project

2.35 : Anurag and Jon on the construction site.

Chapter 2 | Enterprise + Learning

JK	AV + JB

you must deliver to show that it can work and that a community organisation can achieve significant projects and devise original ways of working towards a better future.

Jan: You are not just building homes. Your project deliberately questions the way in which we do housing in the UK. What role does campaigning play? Would you call what you do activism?

Anurag: This is a really interesting question because it goes to the heart of what we do in some ways and the difficulties of it. Kareem was quite clear that there was an educational aspect to the whole thing, right from the start. And this aspect is quite successful. People have come from wide and far. Our school is very successful. But having been through the whole long process, I think that there's a difference between activism and delivery. An organisation that is geared towards lobbying for change has a certain structure. If you have an organisation that is delivering something, it's different. You are constantly being pushed in different directions, as an activist versus as a delivery person. The way that RUSS is doing it is that we have different committees. We want to do it all. We want to reach out to our community because people do come to us and say, how do you do it?

Jan: In a way, you're delivering your proof of concept as you build your argument. I really believe in this symbiotic relationship between driving change and actually delivering change, because it makes it so much more pertinent and believable if you can show off what you've done.

JK	AV + JB

Jon, you have highlighted some of the challenges in your negotiations with the Council. Was there a moment where you felt, this is a big challenge, I don't actually know how to get us out of this?

Jon: I've always felt that anything's possible. It's been difficult, and unnecessarily so for all sorts of reasons, which are to do with the culture in this country as well. I think we are just not that way inclined or haven't been for a long time. Our planning permission, for instance, has 32 conditions and it's ten pages long. The whole risk averse, over-regulated world we live in is difficult to negotiate.

If you talk to the average members of RUSS and you try and explain, they find it quite difficult to understand how complicated it is.

Anurag: I think December 2019 was very, very dark. We had our funding in place and our tenders came back almost £2m over budget. As Chair, I felt responsible. It was almost the end of it. We stopped all the consultants. We battened down the hatches. What was also really sad was that we lost four or five super-engaged residents who had toiled blood, sweat and tears. They had been part of the resident design and the project board. They just couldn't wait any longer. Standing there, I just felt, we've got to get out of this. It took us nearly a year to extricate ourselves from that situation, which meant going back, having to change our lead designers, having to optimise the sizes of dwellings whilst still giving larger than London Plan footprints, adding a few homes, going back to the Greater London Authority for more grant and going back to the bank.

JK   AV + JB

Looking back, we've always had ups and downs. But personally, deep down, I thought, 'We can get through this.' What gave me hope was our biggest asset, goodwill. Whatever might be said about the stakeholders, there is goodwill. The Greater London Authority has goodwill. The banks have a sense of goodwill towards us, and I do think it makes all the difference when things are tough that they give you that extra meeting to talk about it.

It was a step-by-step, small-step, incremental clawing our way back from the precipice. I remember finally signing the construction contract in September 2020. Signing a contract isn't just signing a contract. You have to line up the Greater London Authority. The banks will only sign when you have done that. There's a junior lender and a senior lender. I would say that in November 2020 we were starting to feel confident again.

Jon: It wasn't the first time that we put the brakes on, because at the beginning we ran out of money and we had to shut down, effectively. For me, the early stages were much more exciting. We had 50 people in a room and we said, ok, what do you want? Let's work this out. It was brilliant. Nobody at the time had a clue about the complexities that would follow. There have been compromises along the way, which is inevitable. Sometimes I feel we could have pushed back harder. The energy performance of the dwellings has had to be scaled back.

Anurag: But I think that was also something the residents were given a choice on, right? We said, look, we are scaling back the cost. Would you like homes to have the

2.36 : Self-builders lining the walls of the dwellings. Self-building at Church Grove is not a means to an end, but part of the process of engaging future residents and building community.

JK   AV + JB   JK   AV + JB

Passive House Standard or would you like something that is 20 per cent better than the building regulations, which would be very close, but isn't Passive House, but it'll cost so much less. And the residents were unanimous.

Jon: The rural synthesis is not happening very effectively, because we had to cut out access to the roof for growing and the communal space has been scaled back.

Anurag: But we still retain communal gardens. There will be communal gardening, there will be a communal laundry.

Jon: It's really interesting. I wouldn't say I'm a great admirer of many of the commercial developers in London. But I would say I do understand now, having done this development ourselves, what kind of decisions people need to take to make the sums add up.

Jan: These are tricky decisions. Have you ever felt that there was a conflict of interest between RUSS's simultaneous roles as client/resident, developer and builder? How do you avoid a slow erosion of your ambitions?

Anurag: We have ten principles for a strong neighbourhood which we always keep in the forefront when making decisions. But we also had a commercial imperative. Because if you didn't make those decisions, you're not delivering. The principles were thrashed out in the beginning with the 50 or 100 people we had in our meetings. What does it mean to have a sustainable neighbourhood? We didn't realise at the outset how important it was to get that established right from the off.

Jon: In social housing circles there's a lot of hand wringing about allocations. Everyone gets tied in knots about who should get what and why and how much they should pay for it. The original self-builders in Lewisham had a public meeting where 300 people turned up. And they held a ballot as to who would join the group. We did exactly the same thing.

Jan: Evidently, the lessons learned from your project are complex. But if there were one piece of advice that you could give to another community group embarking on your journey, what would that be?

Anurag: My advice would be very boring. Get organised, be organised, get your vision clear on what you want to do. It's a bit like RUSS's ten principles, almost like a thing you can put in your pocket.

2.37 : Self-builders putting up a partition. The self-building process allows future residents to customise their dwellings to their needs.

2.38 : Planning the works to one of the dwellings. A bespoke approach needed to be designed to apportion liability between the main contractor and the self-builders.

Chapter 2 | Enterprise + Learning

JK　　　AV + JB

I always give this parable of the blindfolded men and the elephant. They want to know the elephant by touch. One holds the tail and says it's a rope, one holds the legs and says it's a tree trunk, one holds the trunk and says it's a thick snake, etc.

When you are a community, it's not about all seeing the same vision. The direction of travel is the same, but what it means to you, what it means to Jon and what it means to me, for example, can be quite different. People do have specific interests. If you want to build an organisation you have to recognise that you are going to get people who have different ideas, characteristics and philosophies but who are committed to going down this route together. The idea that you accept the difference, that people bring, it's really important. Don't think just because you are doing it and I am doing it, we think the same about the same thing. That's where the strength lies, right? In that diversity is also the strength. There are lots of differences of opinion and everybody around you is passionate, they really care. Having the ten principles gives us our direction of travel.

Jon: My advice would be don't be put off by the idea that it's too difficult, takes too long or whatever; by working together, anything is possible; it may be hard, but people who have done it will almost always say that it was really rewarding and well worth it.

Jan: Thank you, Anurag and Jon.

3 / Building + Making

Building and making together have a spatial implication, but my interviewees also work in a sector that can provide training, create jobs, inspire people and bring greater community cohesion. This chapter tells the stories of two projects. Alice Hardy talks about her experience of building Blue House Yard, an enterprise and community project in Wood Green, North London. Rasha El-Sady runs Maxilla Men's Shed, an open-access workshop bringing people in Westbourne Grove, West London, together through making.

Architect Walter Segal (1907–85), mentioned in the previous chapter, is the inventor of the 'Segal Method', an approach to housing design that facilitates self-building. The method was used on social housing developments in Walters Way and Segal Close, Lewisham. The *Architects' Journal* ascribes the architect's legacy to 'an attitude of mind rather than a system of construction'. Segal understood his role very much as an enabler, as he explained: 'We have to give up being experts in one particular field but shall have to learn to assist the vast number of those wishing to participate in the provision of dwellings for themselves.'

Segal managed to achieve much more than creating well-designed homes. He brought home ownership within reach of people who previously never dared to dream they could afford it. Working on-site brought new skills to self-builders, and the communal effort to overcome construction challenges created a tightly knit sense of community which is still alive today, 70 years after the houses were completed.

When Julia King and I set out to design and build the new Skip Garden (see Chapter 1) with 15 undergraduate architecture students at the Bartlett School of Architecture, we were conscious that traditionally educated graduates rarely learn about the social capacity of design and construction processes. Architectural education tends to reward individual excellence, with each student at the end of the year handing in drawings of speculative design projects in response to a brief set by their tutor. The focus is on design per se and rarely on the beneficial by-products that the process can yield when engaging others. Every architect knows that successful architectural practice relies on collaboration and teamwork. At the Skip Garden, students worked on a real site and with a real client. Co-operation and resourcefulness were essential, whilst the ability to engage others was just as important as design excellence. Students graduated having constructed a small building, but they also entered practice with professional and social networks established through their work at the Skip Garden. The project set a new precedent for how architecture can be taught in the UK.

Self-building as an integral part of architectural education is not new. Samuel Mockbee (1944–2001) set up the Rural Studio in 1993, a self-build programme sited in Hale County, Alabama, which is a lasting source of inspiration. Since its inception, Rural Studio students have designed and built over 80 homes and civic buildings for deprived communities in rural Alabama. Experimentation, entrepreneurialism and social responsibility are an integral part of the students' design education.

Self-building starts much earlier than the construction process, however. The Segal Method is based on the skills at hand. At Blue House Yard it was important to think carefully about the scale of building components and the ability of the volunteers. The buildings are constructed entirely in timber, with frames scaled to avoid the need for large construction plant. For a larger communal space, a double-decker bus was bought and converted into a cafe and micro-brewery.

In her interview, Rasha speaks about using hand tools at Maxilla Men's Shed to mitigate workshop noise so that people can speak to each other. Her main objective is to address social isolation. This is done by making together, where participants are prompted to interact when sharing skills, tools and materials. Rasha explains that visitors to Maxilla are in fact very diverse. Those attending come for various reasons: to use equipment, to acquire skills, for social reasons or to become independent and self-sufficient when undertaking DIY tasks at home. Making is the unifying practice that brings the community together across generations, gender and culture, and everybody benefits.

Blue House Yard w/ Alice Hardy

2016 – Present

London, Wood Green, N22

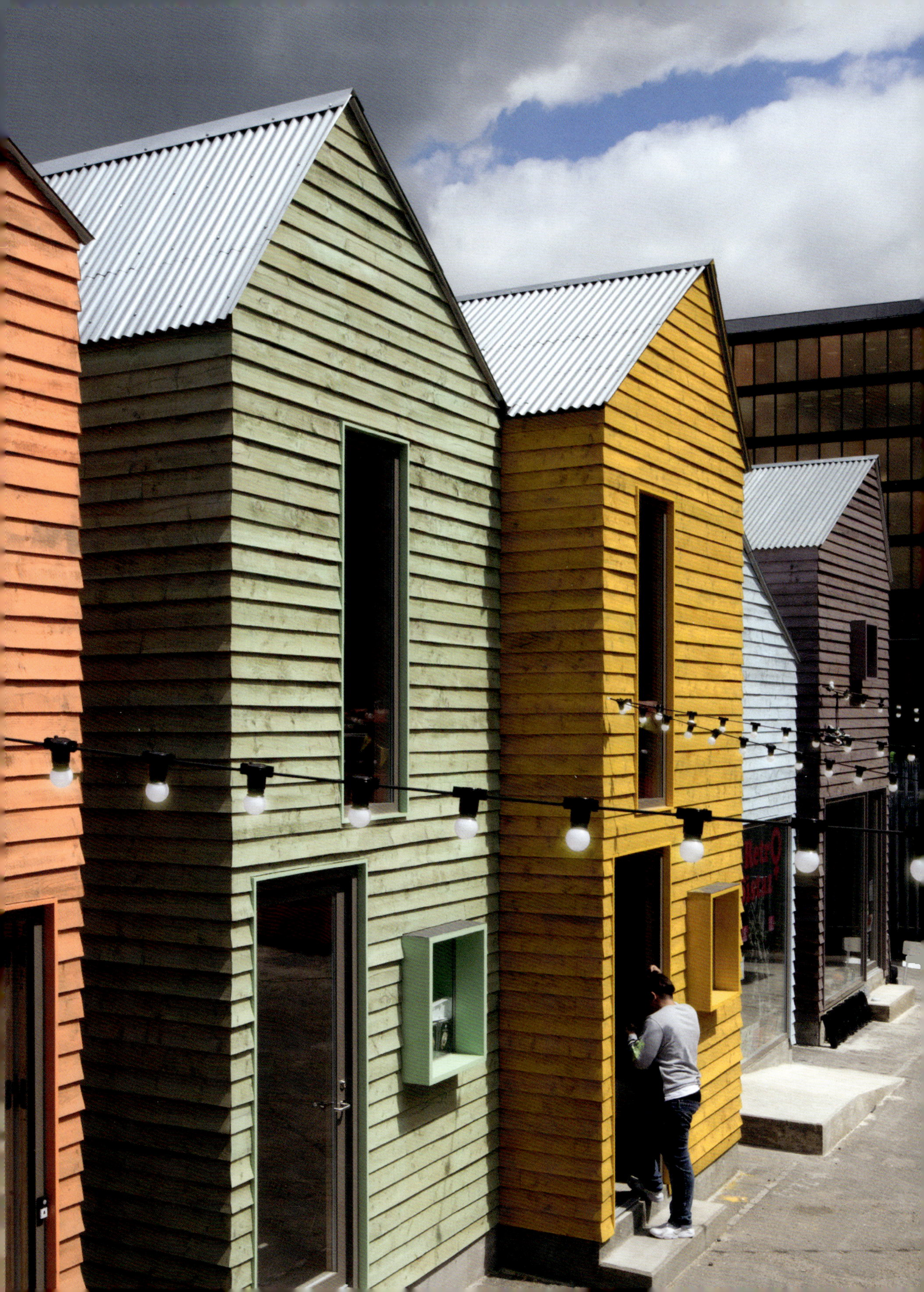

About

Blue House Yard is a collection of temporary micro-workspaces fronting onto a new public square in Wood Green, shaped by collaboration throughout its conception, construction and stewardship. The project provides affordable workspace for 21 small businesses, who employ a total of 50 individuals. The new buildings frame a civic space which is regularly used for community events, markets and performance. The project trained 8 carpentry apprentices and engaged more than 100 volunteers in the construction.

To build Blue House Yard, Jan Kattein Architects and Meanwhile Space Community Interest Company set up their own construction company, High Street Works. This approach had several advantages. With a tenure on-site of just five years, self-building cut out lengthy public sector works-procurement processes eating into a precious and time-limited operational window before the site would be redeveloped with permanent buildings. Managing the construction process internally meant that it could be opened up to stakeholder participation, volunteering and training from day one. Owning construction-related risks and removing the profit margin from the construction phase meant that best value could be retained from a finite funding pot.

The project was initiated by Haringey Council as part of the Meanwhile Campus that sought to establish innovative temporary uses across a number of sites in the town centre. Jan Kattein Architects and Meanwhile Space won the commission to deliver and operate the project through a competitive tender. The Council provided a short-term lease on a vacant car park site and a disused adjacent building. Lease charges are calculated annually on a profit share basis. A linked operator concession obliged High Street Works to design, build and manage workspace, to generate social value and to report regularly to a project board.

Alice Hardy first discovered her passion for making in art class at school, enjoying the immediacy of working with materials but also the social implications that large-scale making has. She had only just graduated from architecture school when an opportunity came up with High Street Works to manage the construction process. She undertook additional training and was then based on-site, managing carpenters, apprentices, builders and volunteers to build Blue House Yard.

Alice's ability to engage and invest others in the project proved pivotal for its realisation. The success of the project is largely due to her personal commitment and sense of purpose. A methodology based on learning by doing galvanised support for the project during construction and created a unique sense of community and belonging that lives on at Blue House Yard today, five years after its completion on-site.

3.01 : [previous page] - The workspace sheds at Blue House Yard. Giving each unit its own front door increased the chance of social interaction and exchange.

Chapter 3 | Building + Making

JK   AH

Jan: How did you decide to study architecture and what got you interested in building?

Alice: I was doing science and maths at college and in art I was building all these sculptures. I had a very influential art teacher. I hadn't really engaged with architecture, but I spoke to him, and we had a discussion about what architecture was. It hadn't really crossed my mind before, that maybe that was something that tied all my interests together. He said, 'I actually think you should do fine art, but if you do want to do architecture I've heard of this school called The Bartlett. Maybe you should check it out.'

Then I came to The Bartlett and found everything really exciting. We were building stuff and I was doing building projects on the side, and everything started to make a whole lot of sense. I was also always interested in communities and social things, the way that people interact with each other. It's funny, that you asked the question 'what made you want to do architecture'. I don't think I was all that sure I still wanted to

3.02 : Alice Hardy, site manager for Blue House Yard.

JK   AH

do architecture when I left undergraduate, and I think every year I question whether it is still something I want to do. But I know I love working in the field, creating spaces and working with people and communities to do things.

Jan: It wasn't by chance that you ended up building Blue House Yard, because that was a line of inquiry that you had already pursued at college. Yet, architects don't normally build things: they draw or write or make models. Wherever there was an opportunity, you would start building. When everyone else was making carefully scaled miniature models, your models at college ended up being big enough to go into.

Alice: I just liked being hands-on. I had done a couple of festival projects during the summer, and at uni I liked the workshop quite a lot. I just found that I like to design through doing, rather than maybe through the computer. But then also I liked the speed of things and the conversations that come around that. When I did get on-site for Blue House Yard, I just really liked the talking to builders and managing things and making it all happen. The kind of social relationships you build with people on-site, those really informal situations, is what really makes things happen. You need to get people motivated and wanting to see that project happen.

Jan: Remind me, how did you get involved in Blue House Yard?

Alice: I think I had come back from building some structures for festivals over the summer. I remember I was going to go travelling, and you said you had an opportunity to manage the construction

133

Londoners Making London

3.03 : Blue House Yard from above. Buildings are framing the new civic square.

Chapter 3 | Building + Making

JK AH

process of Blue House Yard. I was working in the office at the time, and I think I had worked a little bit on the design, and I was like, yeah, I will do that. I just think I was excited by the scheme, but also the process of doing it. It seemed something quite different. I was just really interested in getting hands-on and on-site.

Jan: It was quite a different scale to a festival build, I suppose. An inner-city site, on a car park, publicly accessible, with structures and materials that are bigger than a human being. What preparation did you undertake before you started on-site?

Alice: I went on an accredited course to be a site safety supervisor. Then I also did training as a first aider at work so that I knew the processes for dealing with any kind of accidents on-site. After that, it was a kind of 'learn on the job every day' kind of job. But hands down, I would say it was the team that made it happen – I had amazing carpenters on-site with us. Everyone was helping each other. We had a builder doing different parts on-site and they helped a lot, and there were you and Gabriel Warshafsky explaining what we had to do next.

I would say that a lot of the training happened on the job, and a lot of what I learned was through the people I was working with, who were simply excellent teachers. No one was saying, 'I won't help with that because I am not getting paid for it.' I think the project inspired a lot of people. Even suppliers, like Wood Green Timber, when I told them what we were doing, they just wanted to get our deliveries to site on time. And there was the window supplier who gave us all the windows for free. People could see that this was something exciting

3.04 : The Blue House at night. Painting the existing building blue was one of the first architectural actions on-site, intended to publicly announce the start of the project.

135

Londoners Making London

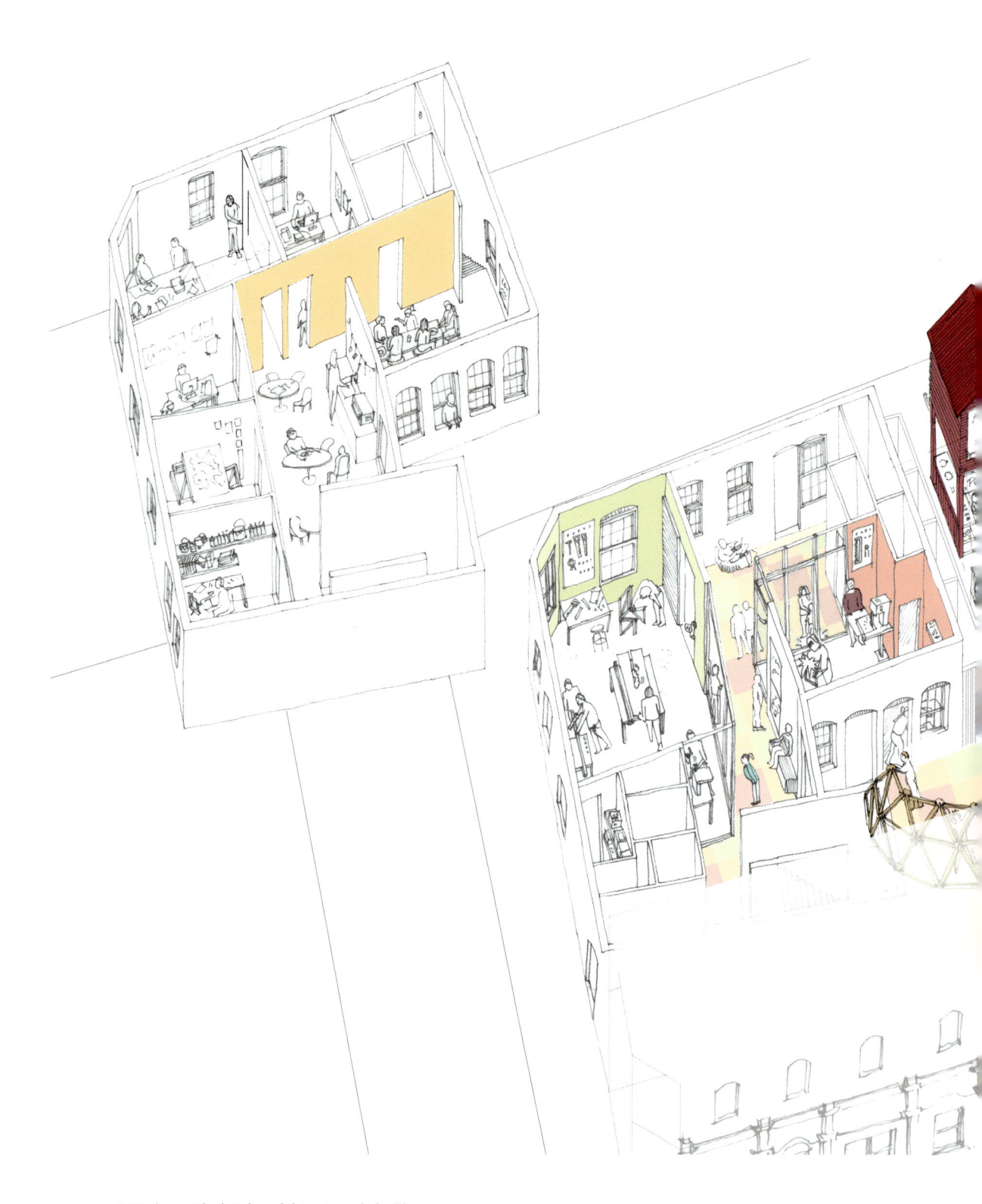

3.05 : Isometric drawing of the proposals for Blue House Yard showing both spaces and activities. The drawing maintained the vision throughout the design and delivery stages.

Chapter 3 | Building + Making

137

JK   AH

and something community oriented and something different. The project attracted so much attention on-site just from passers-by – people were intrigued about what was going on. I think also, a woman wearing a hard hat and high vis with a drill attracted some attention.

Jan: That's interesting: engagement and personal investments seem to have been really important parameters that ultimately made the project happen. Maybe more so than skill and experience. Is that what you'd expected when you started off doing this?

Alice: No, I didn't. And I didn't know. I really didn't know whether I would be successful. I think I felt possibly at the time that you'd put a lot of trust in me. Maybe, I felt underqualified, and I knew it was going to be on a scale that was going to be quite difficult. But when I got on-site, those relationships started to form quickly and we started to work through things. There was a really steep learning curve at the beginning of how we're going to get this project built. And just the day-to-day dramas of working on a site. And then I quickly realised it was about relationships with people and establishing connections and making people want to work for the project.

When the 16-year-old apprentices came to site, that was quite difficult. They did not really want to do the work at first. They just wanted to stand around and look at their phones. But then they saw things happening and they got a bit inspired, and they realised they were actually making things happen. That drummed up more momentum, and then the next day they came ready to start the day. It was just a lot of engagement through the process, I guess.

Jan: What were the moments of crisis?

Alice: I needed to think about this for my exams the other day because there were quite a few moments of crisis. There was a big issue around getting the timber frames up. There were long pieces of timber and we needed to hoist them up. At first, we did it manually, like how you would raise a barn. But then, on days when one of the builders wasn't there, we realised we just didn't have the strength to do that. It needed a lot of strength in numbers, so there were a few moments of trying to get a structure up and then having to get it back down safely.

The other moment of crisis was when Jason, the builder, managed to get his concrete order wrong and they delivered a mound of extra concrete to the site that they refused to take away. So, we ended up having someone break it up with a sledgehammer for about a day and a half, because he had over-ordered the concrete.

Then there was the time when all the windows got delivered and literally filled

3.06 : The disused car park before the project started.

Chapter 3 | Building + Making

3.07 : Putting up the timber frames. The scale and typology of the buildings was conceived so that the frames could be assembled manually and without the need for construction machinery.

Londoners Making London

3.11 : Apprentices from the College of North East London on-site. Opening the project up to the public during the construction phase meant that civic objectives were realised even before the buildings were complete.

Chapter 3 | Building + Making

143

JK   AH

advertisement for the project. People came down whilst we were on-site; potential occupants and people just seemed really interested in the design and the sheds, but they also were interested in the whole process as well. Some of those volunteering on the build became tenants of the completed buildings later. I think it attracted a certain kind of occupant. But I also think that actually the strong part is the design of the space. There's a certain feel around it which you wouldn't get by building it in a conventional way. It's got a human scale to it.

The other thing is the fact that it wasn't super well made – that's not to say it isn't well made, obviously – it means that people feel they can change things and have a greater sense of ownership over the space. I have seen recently that they are painting murals on the Blue House. And people have always decorated their sheds individually.

I feel like we're getting to the point now where the site was going to be developed. Isn't it five years since it opened?

Jan: Actually, they've just extended it by a couple of years.

Alice: The materials obviously weren't made to last forever. But I could see, you know, people themselves just recladding a shed, repainting their shed. It has enough of that informality about it that you could definitely see the community slowly taking over, adding bits, taking bits away, adapting how they use it without being too precious and too rigid.

Jan: How do you see the connection between the learning process and the

3.12 : People on the upper deck of the games cafe. A double-decker bus was a simple and sustainable way of creating enclosed space.
3.13 : Child in bus driver's seat. Retaining many of the elements of the original vehicle creates a quirky interior loved by visitors.

Chapter 3 | Building + Making

JK   AH

opportunity for engagement? You're saying that you were learning on the go. Do you think that that learning on the go was an essential prerequisite to being able to engage so many others to help?

Alice: I think in a way, there was maybe an element of we're doing this for the first time, we're experimenting, we're doing things safely and we're doing things correctly, but we're also learning. Maybe there was a kind of a power in being quite naive and saying, you know, we don't know everything and how this is going to go, and we're actually just working this out. And maybe it did help people to come along with the process. I think people do become more invested when they've had a direct influence on the project.

I think about this with projects that I'm doing now with landscape, and I think sometimes, our structures are so rigid, and what if the local authority could maybe release some control and let the community get involved in constructing some of the spaces? They would then immediately have a direct connection to the space that's being created. Actually, I'm finding that loads of people are looking for opportunities to do that. They really want to be invested in their community. They want to plant the planters outside their house, and they want to create community gardens and they want to be involved, but they need avenues to do that.

I live on an estate, and I had noticed how nice the flower beds were. Then just by chance I walked past a guy who lives in the estate, and he's been doing it for two years and he just does it all off his own bat. There are people out there like that, and if there are projects that galvanise that energy, then

3.14 : Volunteer painting one of the worksheds.

3.15 : [next page] The yard is the social heart of the project and it provides for flexible and temporary uses such as markets and seasonal celebration.

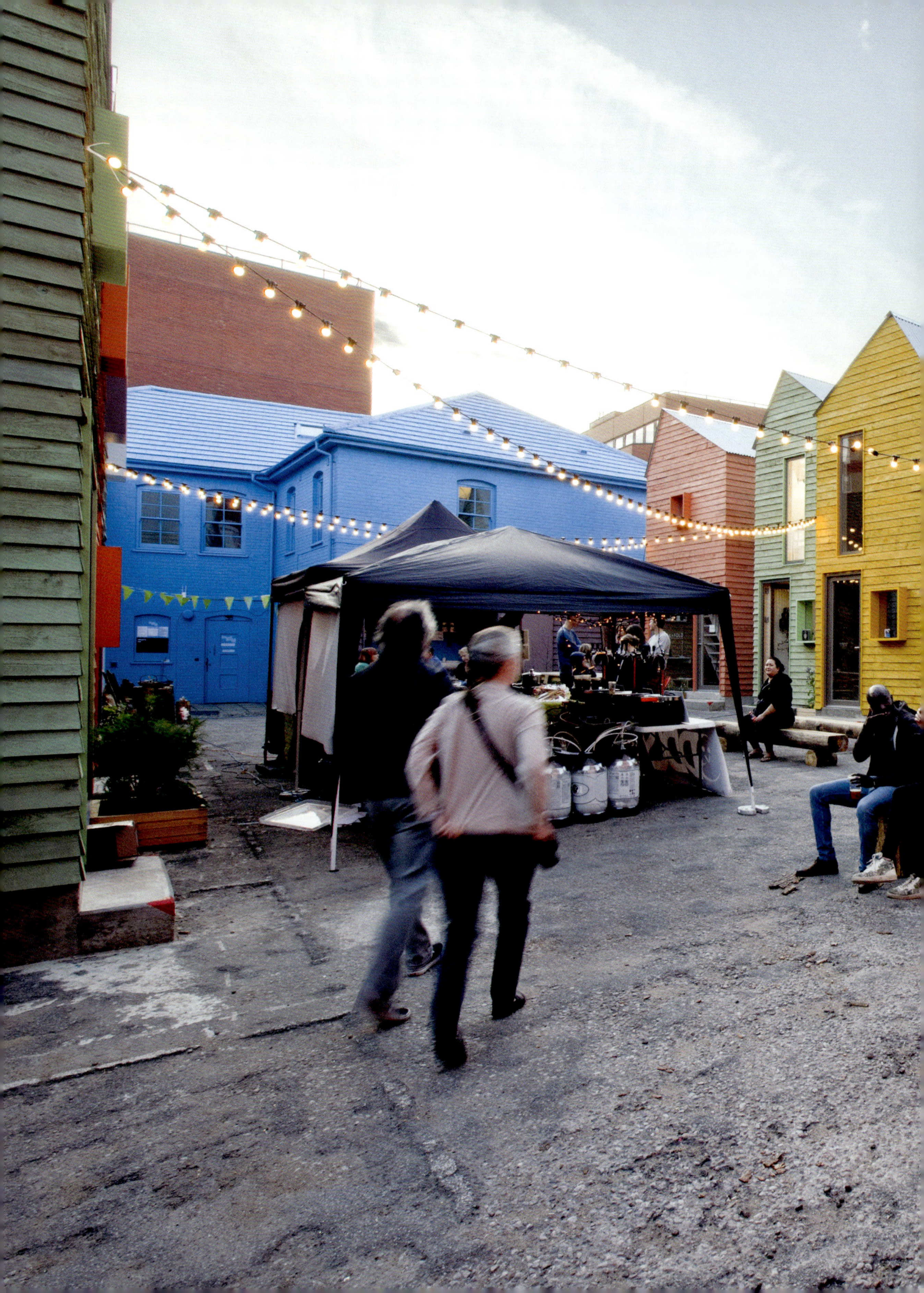

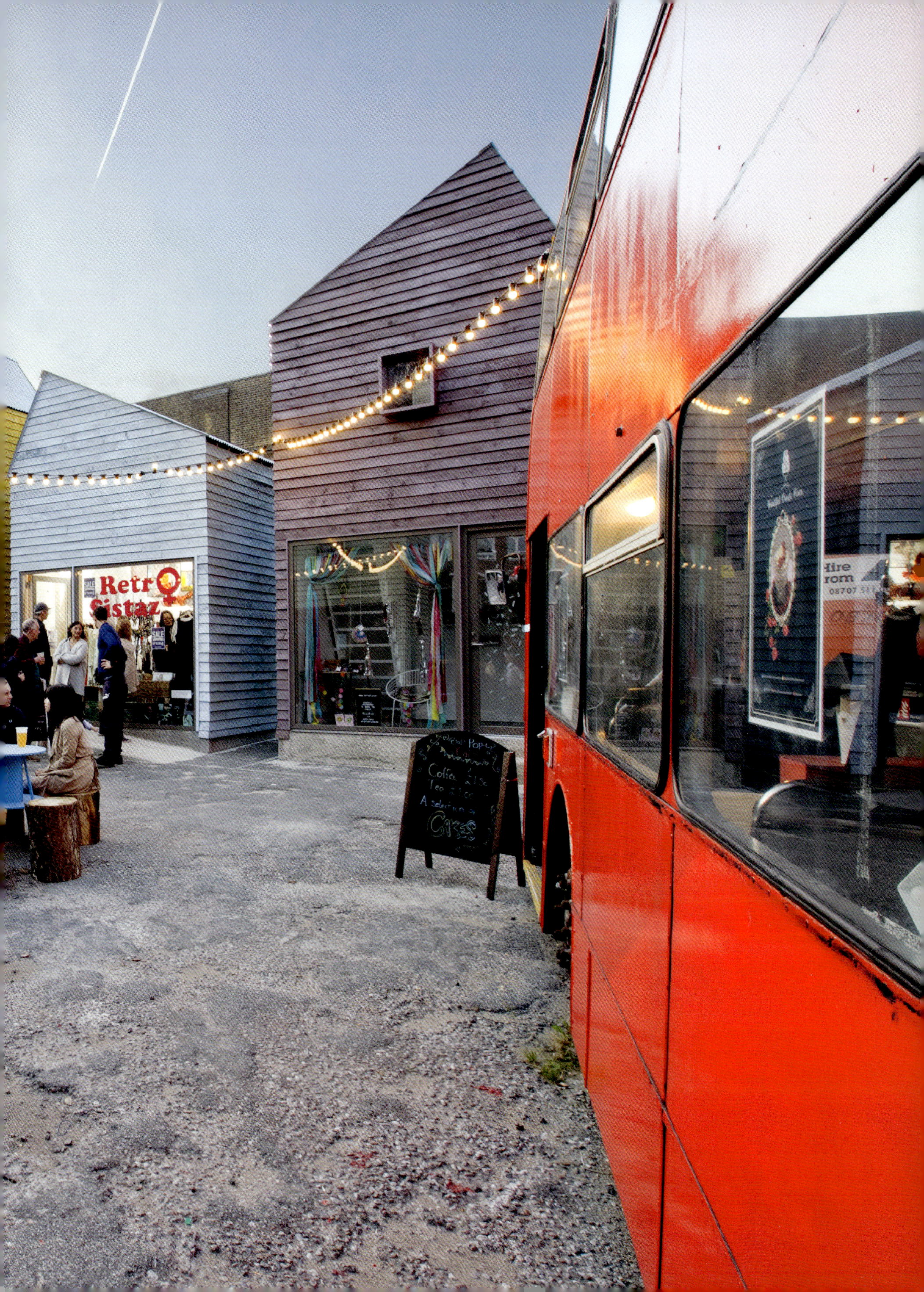
Retro
Sistaz
Coffee

JK AH

you do get loads of people that want to be involved. Maybe I will get in touch with the guy that's doing all the gardening and maybe we'll try and create a community garden on the estate – there's loads of space and it's not being used for anything.

Jan: Do you think that architects in particular have the opportunity to impact through their practice?

Alice: Having built Blue House Yard, I would say that I can see often, when I'm doing projects now, that there's an alternative solution. And sometimes I get a little bit disheartened if I do a project and I could imagine how it could be. We could have such a massive impact if we didn't stick to such traditional building procurement processes. I find that sometimes frustrating.

Clients want to just see the project happen in the process that they're used to; they don't want a risk and they don't want to get out of that comfort zone in a way. I think sometimes when I'm doing a project, we could involve this organisation and that. But you do just hit brick walls, with people unwilling to do things a little bit differently and involve more people.

I'll be at engagement events, and I see people literally offer time. I see people say, 'I'd like to be involved in this further, I want to do this.' And, because of the procurement processes or because of the way the project's been set up, there's no avenue for involving them. It's not even resources. Councils often do not have the structures in place that allow them to do these kinds of projects. I feel if architects thought a bit more out of the box, then we could do projects that are different. Especially with

3.16 : Resident entrepreneurs in their workspaces. The worksheds were particularly popular with retailers, designers or makers who were selling online but still wanted a high street presence.
3.17 : [ibid]

Chapter 3 | Building + Making

3.18 : Gallerist in front of his workspace. The rental terms made it simple to move in and also simple to move out.

design and build, these projects often have half as much of an impact as they could.

Blue House Yard was probably quite exhausting physically and we spent a lot of cold mornings in January building outside, but I would never not have done it because of that; it was just really exciting and, and fun.

Jan: When did it occur to you that you were doing something that has inspired hundreds, if not thousands, of people?

Alice: It was definitely when we started working with the construction college and you saw this kind of change in those teenage boys. Them turning from, 'What is this? Why are you trying to make me do this kind of thing?' to then becoming genuinely invested. And some of them were like, 'Can I come back at the weekend and help?'

I went back and did some post-occupancy interviews with occupants for a report I was writing at university at the time. It was amazing how everyone described being there and just how much of a community had evolved around it. Some people have asked me to give talks about working as an architect on-site and my role at Blue House Yard. And then people come to speak to me afterwards and they say, 'Oh, you know, I live around there', or 'I go for a drink there on an evening and go to the weekend market', and 'My kid did this and that' – there's loads of kids' activities going on now. It seems like a place that has a bit of a buzz around it. But I wouldn't put that down to me. I would put it down to everyone that was involved in the whole process.

Jan: Thank you, Alice.

3.19 : The bus was shared by two businesses, Cakes and Ladders and the Earth Tap Brewery. This kept cost down for both and ensured that the yard remained active during the day and at night.

Chapter 3 | Building + Making

3.20 : Pop-up cafe in the bus. To find a tenant for the bus, the space was initially let on a short-term basis, giving entrepreneurs the opportunity to trial their business before committing for the long term.
3.21 : The upper deck of the bus.

Maxilla Men's Shed w/ Rasha El-Sady

2019 – Present

London, North Kensington, W10

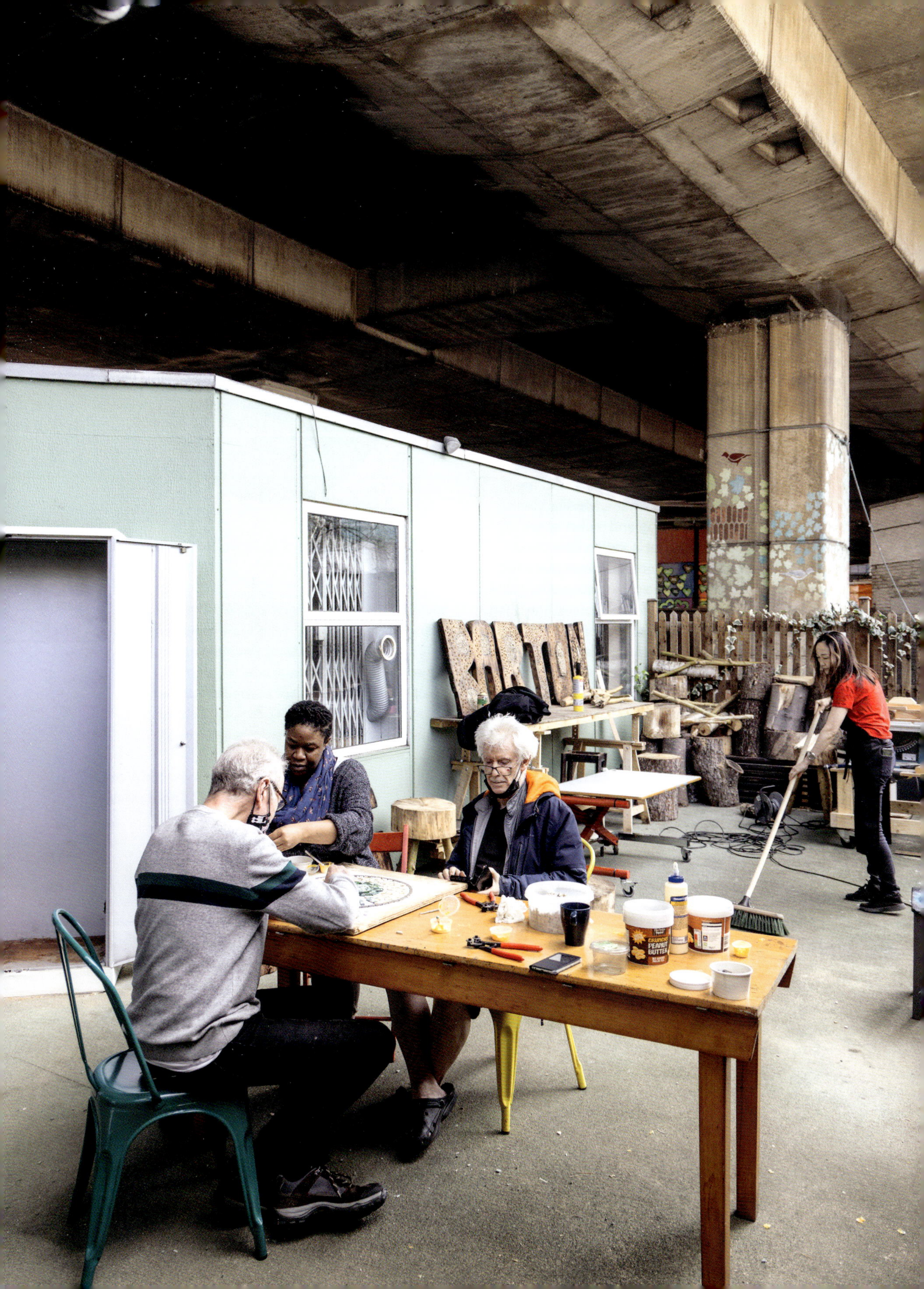
CRUNCHY
PEANUT
BUTTER

Londoners Making London

3.24 : Coat rack outside the workshop.

Chapter 3 | Building + Making

JK   RE-S

Jan: Tell me more about the people who come to the Shed.

Rasha: I've tried to make the Shed as accessible as possible. There are a lot of different people who come – men, women and a range of ages – for a variety of reasons. For example, we have young people who come because they want to be self-sufficient and learn how to use a drill, and we'll show them all the different drills and settings and wall types and plugs and screws. Or another example is some retired carpenters who've been making bespoke cabinets for most of their lives and who get a lot of value from sharing their knowledge and skills. They enjoy advising others about techniques, problem solving and looking after the tools. Those are the things they love doing. Having a variety of people there gives them that space to interact and to feel free from any label as to why they are here. It works well having everybody around.

Jan: You are in a very diverse part of London. How do you make sure that what you offer appeals to a range of communities?

Rasha: It's not about the programme offer or the course content, but about the environment we create. Making a space which is safe, inviting and welcoming, and being a great place for everyone. It's not just woodworking. That's what I like to emphasise. We have makers, we have graffiti street artists – there is such a variety of what you can do. We talk about the socialising aspect. You don't have to make, you can just come and have a look and enjoy a cup of tea. There is absolutely no pressure to make anything; I want it to be whatever you want it to be. If we can

3.25 : Shedder showing their work.

157

3.26 : Mosaic-making at the Shed as part of the Grenfell relief effort.

JK RE-S

accommodate you or your ideas, we will. In my experience those barriers start to slowly shift.

Jan: How about your role as a woman running a Men's Shed? Have you experienced any challenges associated with this? Or are there opportunities that you have been able to embrace?

Rasha: I've worked in the making industry for a long time; carpentry and bespoke fitouts specifically can be quite male-dominated in certain aspects. What I find is that I have to explain why it's called the 'Men's Shed', the link with the Men's Shed movement and how our model works. The fact that I'm a woman running the project perhaps helps demonstrate that it's genuinely a space for everyone.

Jan: Your role is really quite central to the success of the project. You are local and have grown up in the neighbourhood. That's special. How does that play into the project?

Rasha: I guess it helps in a certain way. I have grown up with the people in this area and I understand my community and the environment. You start to identify with certain struggles or certain stories that you can relate to. I also know from my own experience as a young creative with a young family, moving into my first flat – a blank canvas with limited resources – that I could've really benefited from having a local setup like Maxilla Men's Shed for support.

Jan: How about your educational background? Has that given you any particular skills or insight that is now integral to what you do?

JK RE-S

Rasha: 100 per cent. I did an Art and Design foundation and then a BA in Visual Communication Design. There was a process that we had to follow for every project brief we received. I followed this process non-stop for three years on all my projects.

Before managing the Shed I was doing a lot of teaching, including with the young makers at the Victoria & Albert Museum and at a community interior design college. I would always be very strict about the brief; it should answer all your questions. It's also what makes the difference between being out of pocket or the job paying for itself. I know my strengths and weaknesses in this process very well. My strengths have always been linking what the client needs to what the community wants, and the development process. I bring that to the Shed every day.

Jan: The Shed does much more than Tinkering Sessions and workshops. You are building a network with other organisations to give those coming to the Shed, and their work, a purpose. You have also been involved in commissioning artwork for the hoardings around the Shed. Why does engaging with the city around you matter? Or was this always part of your job description?

Rasha: I see the benefits of creativity everywhere. I look for opportunities and am always thinking about what next and what more. It gives people something to look forward to, and there is an opportunity for change. I'd love to build a skatepark next to the Shed. I want to learn how to make skateboards and I want the Shedders to develop the process and make them. I'd love to see young people then work with graffiti

JK   RE-S

artists to design the artwork on the boards with collaboration between the generations. It's not in my job description, but ACAVA supports a lot of my creative ideas. In my experience, there is something different at ACAVA: the people who work there, they are also creatives and support creativity.

Jan: Maybe the reason that the Shed is so well loved is because it provides space for creativity. You have occupied a niche in an ever more regimented world. As an architect working in urbanism, what I am really keen to understand is what one might learn from the Shed that could inform the way that we build cities.

Rasha: It's about creativity, but it's also about continuity and longevity, especially within a funding context. It's so important to me to create the security from which we can build trust and relationships with the participants, which is what makes it genuine. If you're struggling with social isolation and loneliness, it can take you days to leave your bed to come to the Shed for five minutes. So having something where people are just starting to get comfortable, where they trust you, where they feel they can put strategies in place to cope, it's important to know we are going to be there next week and the week after.

We know that creativity is good for your mental health and well-being. It's so important to be making. We know all the research that supports this. Creativity is the foundation, but it's more than that: it's a way for people who are not comfortable being around each other to break those social boundaries. They end up working on the same workbench together with others and then ask: 'Do you know what this tool

3.27 : Shedder carving.

Chapter 3 | Building + Making

JK RE-S

does?' or 'Do you know the best saw to use for this?' or 'I'm working with wood and you're working with mosaics, do you think I could create a wooden frame for this?' It's a gradual process which doesn't work well when it's short term.

This is why I feel the Shed is working, because people know we're open every week all year long. I combine that permanence with lots of exciting little things that create new opportunities for Shedders and new social and community interactions. We ran a Black History Month event with an artist and musician in the outside space of the Shed, which many Shedders attended. Another example is a project we took part in with a local artist to make sculptures for public spaces in and around our community, which really highlighted the intergenerational dynamic to the Shed. Some of our older male Shedders were out

3.28 : Shedders working together. Coming to the Men's Shed is about having a sense of worth and about socialising and being with others.

JK RE-S

of their comfort zone and stood back and observed some of the younger Shedders lose their inhibitions whilst creating bold, abstract, messy and colourful designs. Within just a short time, they started to feel inspired by these designs and take part in the process.

Jan: What were the challenges? And what were the highlights? And what if somebody wanted to set up a similar sort of project? What would your advice be?

Rasha: I don't think there's a simple answer. My advice would be to challenge the ways we are expected to do things – if it doesn't make sense to you, question it. One idea when setting up the Shed was to have a lot of large machines; however, in a workshop with machines – whether they are being operated or not – you need to wear ear defenders. How can you socialise with ear defenders on? We all agreed that having a focus on hand tools would be a much better way to create an environment for everyone to enjoy making whilst socialising.

And ask why – question the process. I have attended events where the struggle to engage more men in activities is a reoccurring topic being discussed. Maybe it's some of the processes, the forms and the surveys that we ask them to complete, and the uncomfortable labels that come with that. Maybe that's incompatible with how that particular demographic you're trying to engage likes to do things. There's a lot of evaluation. I get it, because funders need to measure the impact of their funding and we need to prove our projects work, but I would say challenge the way it's done and look at more creative ways of getting those outcomes. We have worked to do this in

3.29 : [next page] Shedders working together.

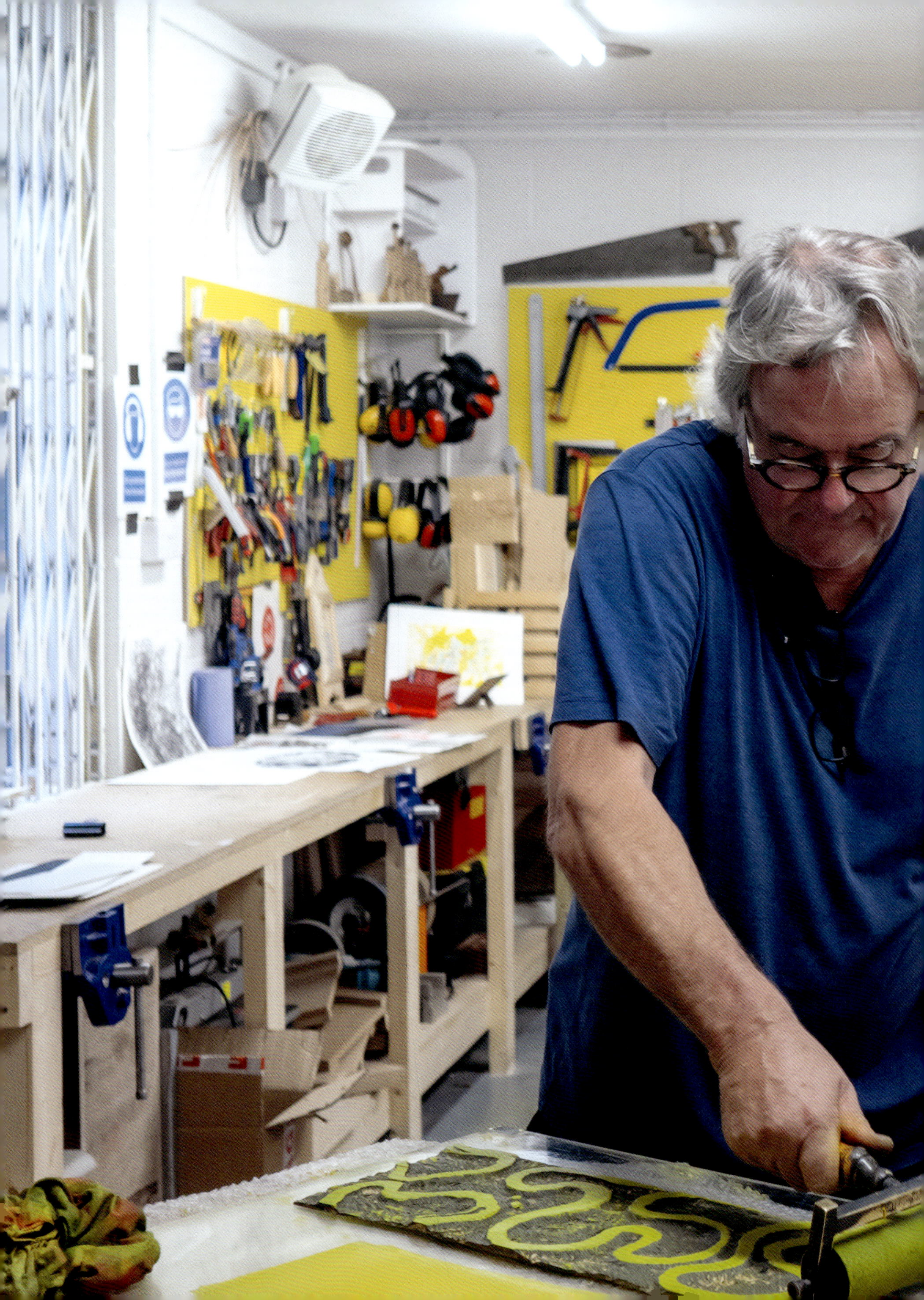

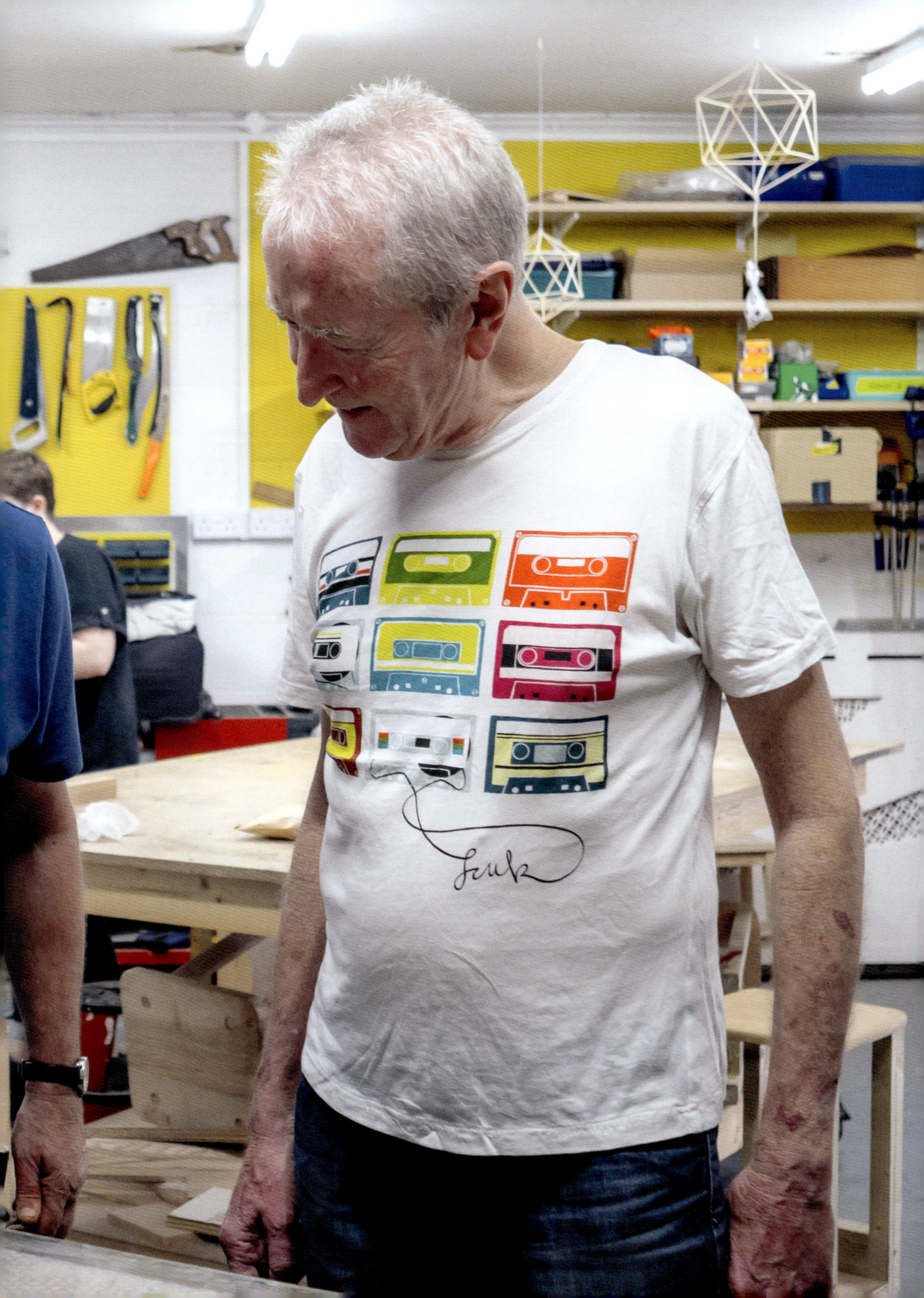

JK   RE-S

    the Shed and it's removed some barriers to taking part. I would really like to shift the current process of allocating funding which means you have to commit to an idea and what you are going to evaluate before you have even received the money or started the project in a very inflexible way.

Jan: It's interesting that you're saying this. We're struggling with this all the time as creative practitioners. In order to be accountable to a community, you've got to commit to a journey with an unknown outcome. And if you don't, then you're not being genuine, in a way.

    Rasha: I'm also struggling with that. You have to provide quantitative targets of what you're going to achieve; you might achieve much more, but you might also achieve something very different or you could achieve nothing. It also means you have to stick to one agenda and aren't able to change based on the service user, on what you observe during a project. Something needs to change there. We're always looking at solving a problem – we never talk about prevention. We wait until you have a mental health crisis and then we're like, what can we do? This is relevant to the Maxilla Men's Shed and why our model is not just about older people. What if younger people want to get involved? Would we really say no to them? Why can't this be seen as prevention? That's what's nice to see at the Shed: there's also a young generation learning and experiencing community. Stories about people are more powerful than statistics.

Jan: Thank you, Rasha.

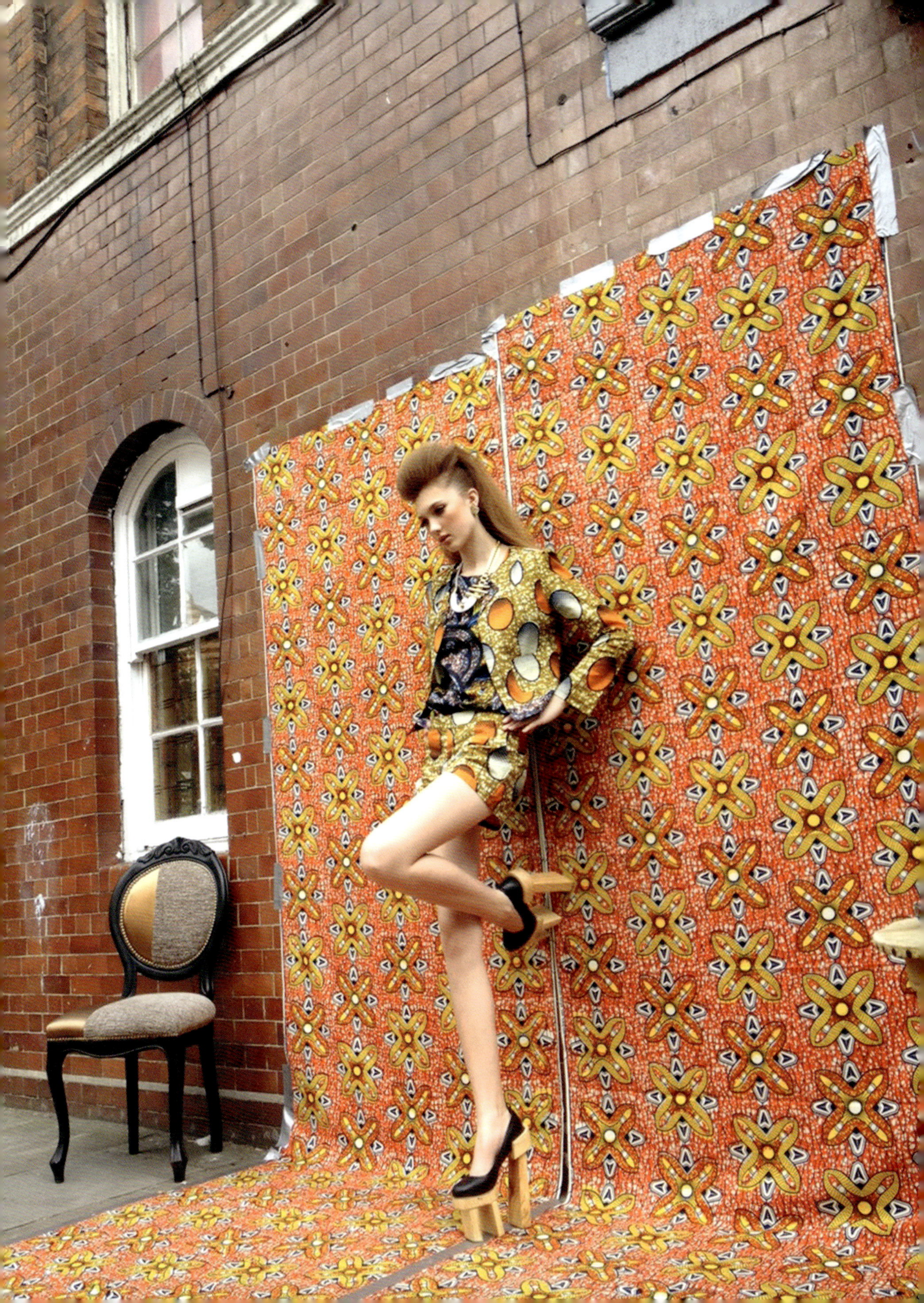

About

The African Street Style Festival took place in Calvert Avenue in East London in 2013. It was a small gathering of about 200 people. When Jeffrey organised a sequel in 2015, the success defied all expectations. Thousands of people took over the street that had been closed to cars and transformed into a place of creativity and cultural expression.

For just a day, African Street Style promotes togetherness and cultural exchange whilst quietly advocating for the permanent re-balancing of public urban space to give greater priority and a sense of ownership of the street to people.

The setting of African Street Style is significant. Calvert Avenue forms part of the Boundary Estate, which was constructed from 1890. The estate was the earliest social housing scheme built by the London County Council. The buildings are five-storey, red-brick tenement blocks arranged along streets that radiate from a central square, Arnold Circus. The Boundary Estate is a protected heritage asset celebrated for its social and civic significance.

Jeffrey Lennon is an urbanist and regeneration professional who lives and works in London. When after the London Olympics he perceived a real desire from communities to become creatively engaged with their neighbourhoods, Jeffrey had the idea of organising a festival that would take over Calvert Avenue. He went on to mobilise creative practitioners, performers and musicians, local residents and retailers. He secured funding, undertook marketing and obtained licences.

Jeffrey's background as an urbanist has shaped both conception and programming. His family history and his interest in the African diaspora has informed the festival theme. The programme championed participation rather than mere observation of other people and the urban environment. African Street Style can also be understood as a form of guerrilla urbanism where citizen action pilots alternative ways of shaping our cities and engaging with each other and our urban spaces.

4.01 : [previous page] Model in public photography studio set up on pavement.

Chapter 4 | Temporality + Activation

JK   JL   JK   JL

Jan: Jeffrey, tell me about African Street Style. How did you come up with the idea?

Jeffrey: I think with any initiative which brings together places and spaces and how we utilise them, especially in a creative and artistic form, there are always quite a few things which come together to make that happen.

We go back to 2012, around the time when the London Olympics had just finished. There was a feeling that people began to celebrate the city in a slightly different way. I think I recognised subconsciously that there was a demand from local people outside professional circles to engage more, find out more, participate more in the places where they live. This was probably inspired by policy and outreach that promoted localism. I think African Street Style came from that underlying recognition that local people wanted to participate in local life in a different way.

As for the location of African Street Style, it's located in Calvert Avenue, which forms part of the Boundary Estate, a historic residential neighbourhood with some retail along small streets. This intimate, resilient retail cluster is very important, as in many ways it facilitates the people/street association. It also reflects and retains the original objectives and ambitions of the Boundary Estate, namely the intention to introduce artisans, makers, craftspeople to the area.

However, there was no expression, there was no formal platform for people to engage with that. And what I was thinking was, well, what we need to do here is think about how we can reimagine a place like this so people can begin to celebrate this area. How can we utilise all this to create something which is liberating, something which is fun, something which is expressive, but appropriate for the space. Also, in many places, people need to work their lifestyles around the car, and I wanted to challenge that, and I thought African Street Style was a good way of doing so.

Jan: That's really interesting. There are many other sites in London that you could have chosen. What was it that made you choose Calvert Avenue?

Jeffrey: Pragmatism is also in the mix. I knew a number of the retailers at Calvert Avenue, and they supported my idea. I work in urbanism and am interested in the places in which we live and how the associations between people, places and businesses function. And then there was the historic Boundary Estate. It was a brilliant concept, socially and politically progressive. It was built in response to a terrible condition with very, very poor people living in squalor, and a progressively thinking administration at the time brought

4.02 : Jeffrey Lennon, Founding Director of African Street Style.

4.03 : [next page] Dancing on the street at the African Street Style festival.

173

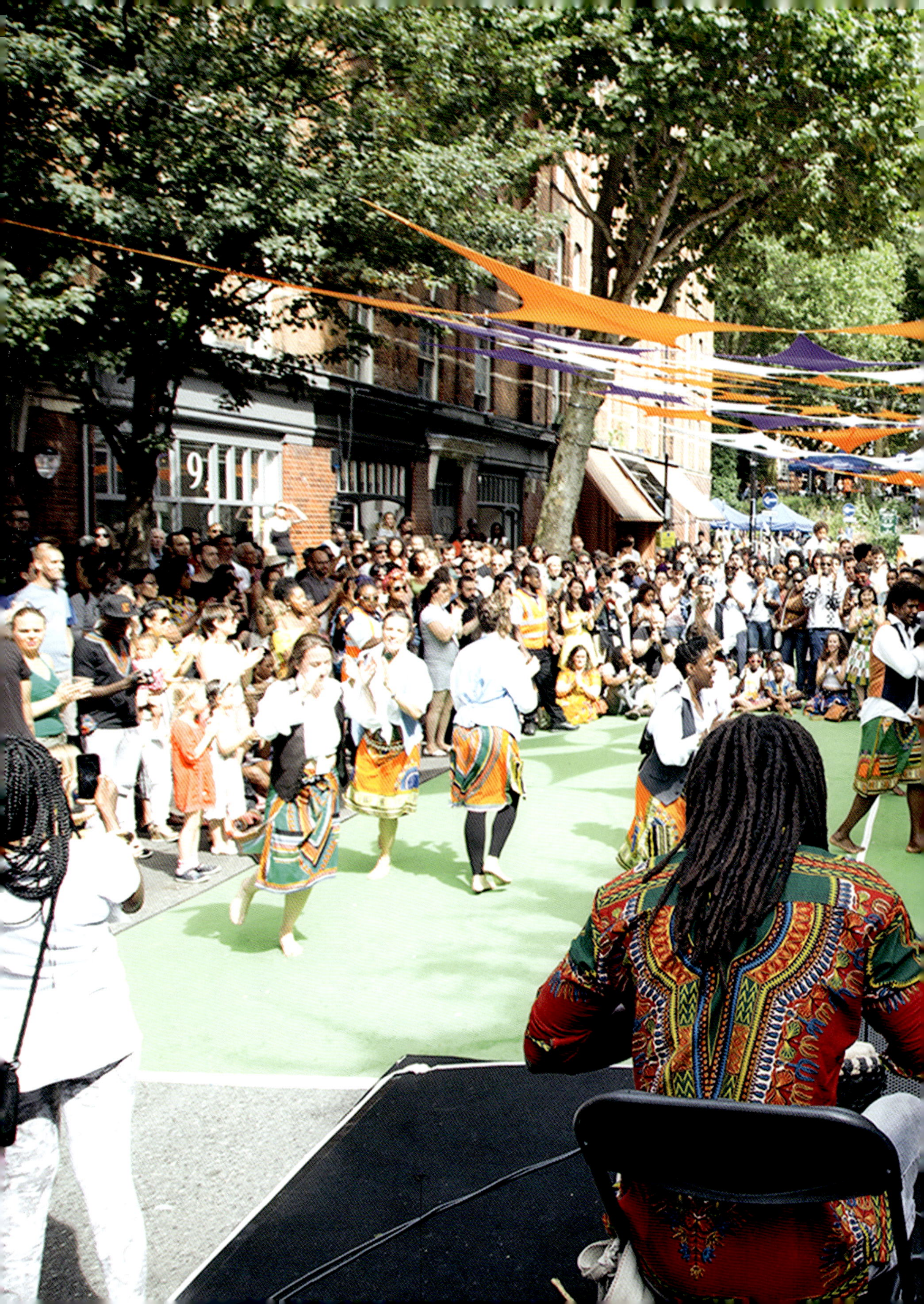

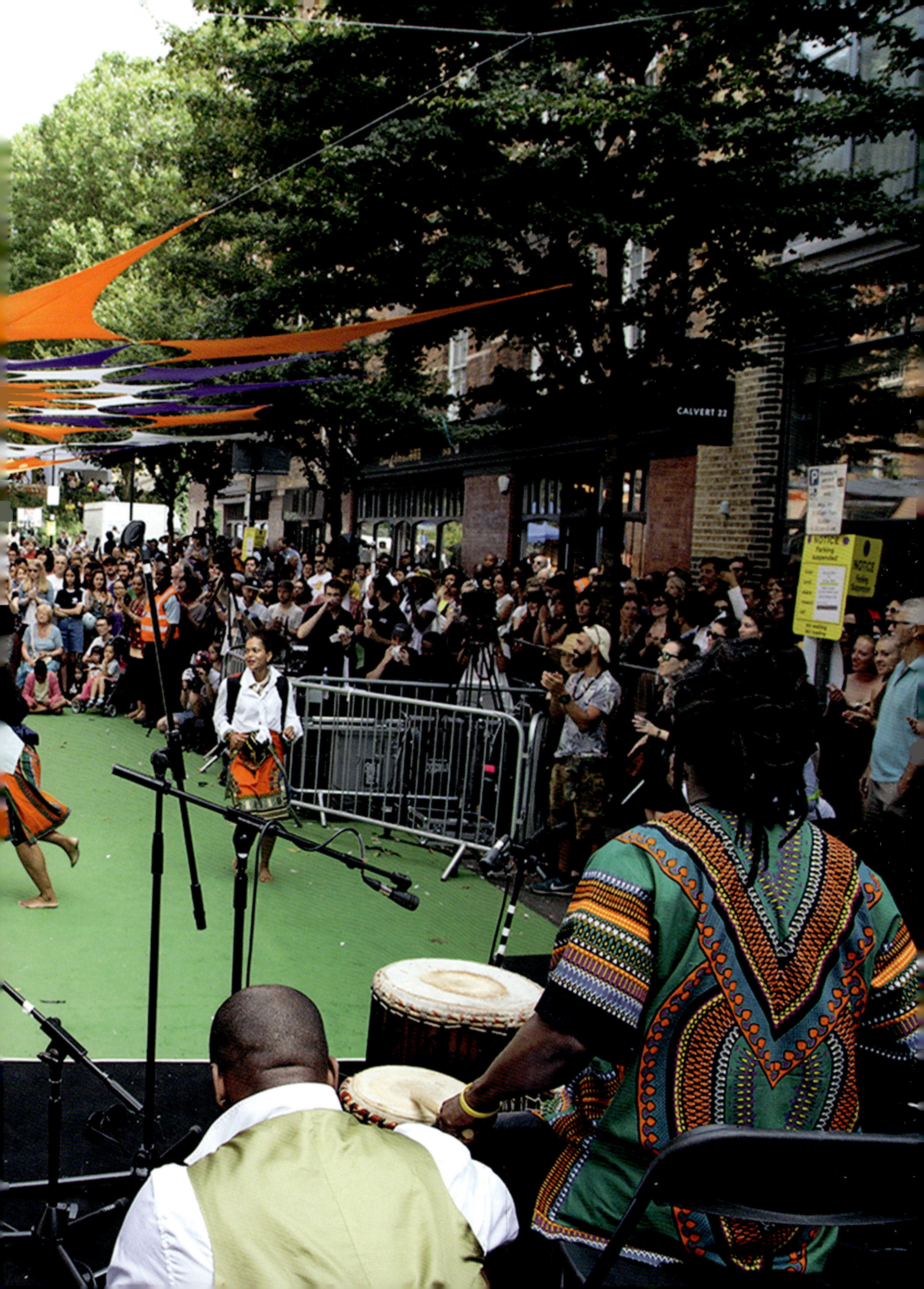
CALVERT 22

JK   **JL**

JL: in an architect to completely reimagine the area. I am not sure that that would happen today, with such a bespoke approach being taken to the architecture, and such a radical approach to social policy through urban design. Remember this was the first council estate, and the most expansive project of its kind attempted under the Housing of the Working Classes Act 1890. So that's a beautiful backdrop to African Street Style. That's important, because I think one of the things that made me feel confident and comfortable to base a festival with arts, music, performance, fashion and photography there is that it's about people. Bringing people together, without commercial interest creating a meeting destination. In fact, as you know, the Arnold Circus was essentially built to serve this purpose. The buildings across the Boundary Estate are 100 foot high, immediately creating this beautiful theatre for communal gathering. Not all street festivals are able to do this, provide a natural, quite definitive historic and architectural setting, but this one certainly does.

There is a photographer down there, on Calvert Avenue, Hassan Hajjaj, a Moroccan, who has a delightful shop called Larache. He is based there, and occasionally curates these little photography sessions, on the pavement outside his store. He basically gets one of these Moroccan-style mats, some Sellotape, nothing more, and he would fix the mat to the wall and take pictures of people in front of it. What I always found interesting in that, was that it wasn't just about the photography, it wasn't just about his eye for detail. This was about a local person utilising the beauty of the built environment around him to create that sense of destination, to create that space

JK   **JL**

where people, not just local people, but personalities, celebrities, wanted to be.

Jan: So Hassan's practice set the theme for the festival?

Jeffrey: There was Hassan, but there was also another proprietor, Samson Soboye, a West African stylist. He produces quite high-end clothing and furnishings which are informed by his heritage. He has a brilliant mind, a very effervescent guy who lectures at Central Saint Martins. Both of these people came together, and I remember having a conversation with them, sitting in the middle of Calvert Avenue, and I said listen, we've got the perfect platform here to bring what you do out into the street and invite people to interact with it and celebrate it.

We took a lot of photography at the first event in 2013. I was convinced that if we could get a critical and robust set of imagery which we can show people, we can say: this is what happens when you take time out to get to know a local area, to get to know the local community, to get to know the local retailers, and when you celebrate the beauty of London's history and architecture. And if we brought all that together, we could get people to see, that's the sort of thing we want to encourage more of in our public spaces. Remember, the UK has a very strong tradition of hosting street parties!

Jan: African Street Style as a form of activism, a campaign?

Jeffrey: The promotional narrative was key, very simple, open and in many ways unequivocable. People understood, 'I'm going to be able to be there by literally

Chapter 4 | Temporality + Activation

4.04 : Dancer with ankle bells.

Londoners Making London

4.07 : Model in public studio.

JK   JL

That's significant, unnecessary and a very sad reflection of a wider psychology which besets aspects of our lives, in my opinion. We have never had any trouble of any kind at our festivals. None. That isn't luck, that's true stakeholder partnership, a result of what happens when you empower people in a responsible way.

Jan: Despite these challenges, African Street Style has been a massive success. When did you realise just how big it was?

Jeffrey: For the first edition, I didn't have much resource to play with. And that was fine. We had no fundraising strategy. It was me, driving this concept through, with the intention of really testing the market, testing the model. I wanted it to evolve, grow, really organically, because that's how you identify efficiencies, and highlight the aspects of the event which require focus. So, Samson Soboye, who we commissioned to pull together a fashion shoot, got his models in. He got these beautiful outfits ready and I said, look, when you get your make-up artists in, they're going to do their make-up in the middle of the street. People are going to be able to watch practitioners at work. How do you do make-up? What does it look like? What do you use? Why do you use that? Speak to the make-up artists, speak to the models, speak to the stylists, speak to the photographers. It's our space. That's what we wanted to do. Challenge convention. I bought 100 m of Astroturf and laid this out, called on some family and friends to help with the logistics. And we had a couple of acoustic musicians, it was beautiful. We didn't have the money to get a big system or anything like that, and we did not want anything like that. Not yet. One of my brothers had an old sound system and I

JK   JL

said, come along, we'll rack it up, we'll get some microphones or whatever, and it just worked perfectly. And I think we knew when all that came together, it looked beautiful and it was a bit higgledy-piggledy, but we all knew at that time, it was exactly what it was supposed to be. We were working it out, of course, but we had something at the end of that day because it looked beautiful and everyone was thinking, 'This is a bit different, but this really works.'

The pilot in 2013 provided the platform for the 2014 edition, which attracted two and a half thousand people. And we had a bit of a stage, a bit of a catwalk, but we never lost that sense of, well, it's still about local people. We utilised our networks, remained humble, retained the scale. We didn't want to increase the area of the festival.

Jan: To what extent do you think that your personal background and upbringing has shaped African Street Style?

Jeffrey: My parents were from Jamaica, they're from the Windrush Generation. They came over here in the late 50s, early 60s. They raised their family, a very humble, but very fun beginning. I am one of six children. Community and thinking of others, that's always been built into me, and I think that's a cultural thing. That's something that is part of my heritage because I know that's how my parents were raised. I am also genuinely interested in the African diaspora. Who you are and what your true roots are is of critical importance and interest to me. I think about where such thinking, of essentially historic, consistent migrant movement reflects across London. Music was a constant theme and a memory of my upbringing, I realise it now why they used to listen to

Londoners Making London

4.08 : Street used as public space.

4.09 : Street used as public space.

4.13 : Design for African Street Style by Anna Mill.

JK   JL

need for us to sensibly and appropriately scrutinise authorities, institutions and the private sector to keep questioning how we all want to live. Most of our lives are spent locally, and I don't know whether it's imagination or the sheer will to persuade a local authority to open up and liberalise how the public can use public space. So maybe in some ways I do think that's a form of activism, and I suppose it's activism in the sense that I knew that I had to win, rather than just make that argument.

One of the issues, I think, is that local authorities find it difficult to know where their role stops. And then whose role is it to make these types of events happen? Should the local authority manage street festivals? Or do they trust local people? And I think at the moment there isn't a definitive answer to that question, and that creates a gap. However, the fact that African Street Style is not a Council event makes a significant difference.

It's democratic, it's free, it's liberal, it's about people, and the backdrop is the outstanding architecture and fascinating history that this great city can offer. And people have shown we can come together and do something that's wonderful. And, you know what's really interesting? That way of thinking, that idea, that concept, it doesn't require a quantum leap in thinking, it's just that we need to learn to normalise that.

Jan: Thank you, Jeffrey.

Food Bus w/ Kemi Akinola

2020 – Present

London, Wandsworth, SW18 (and beyond)

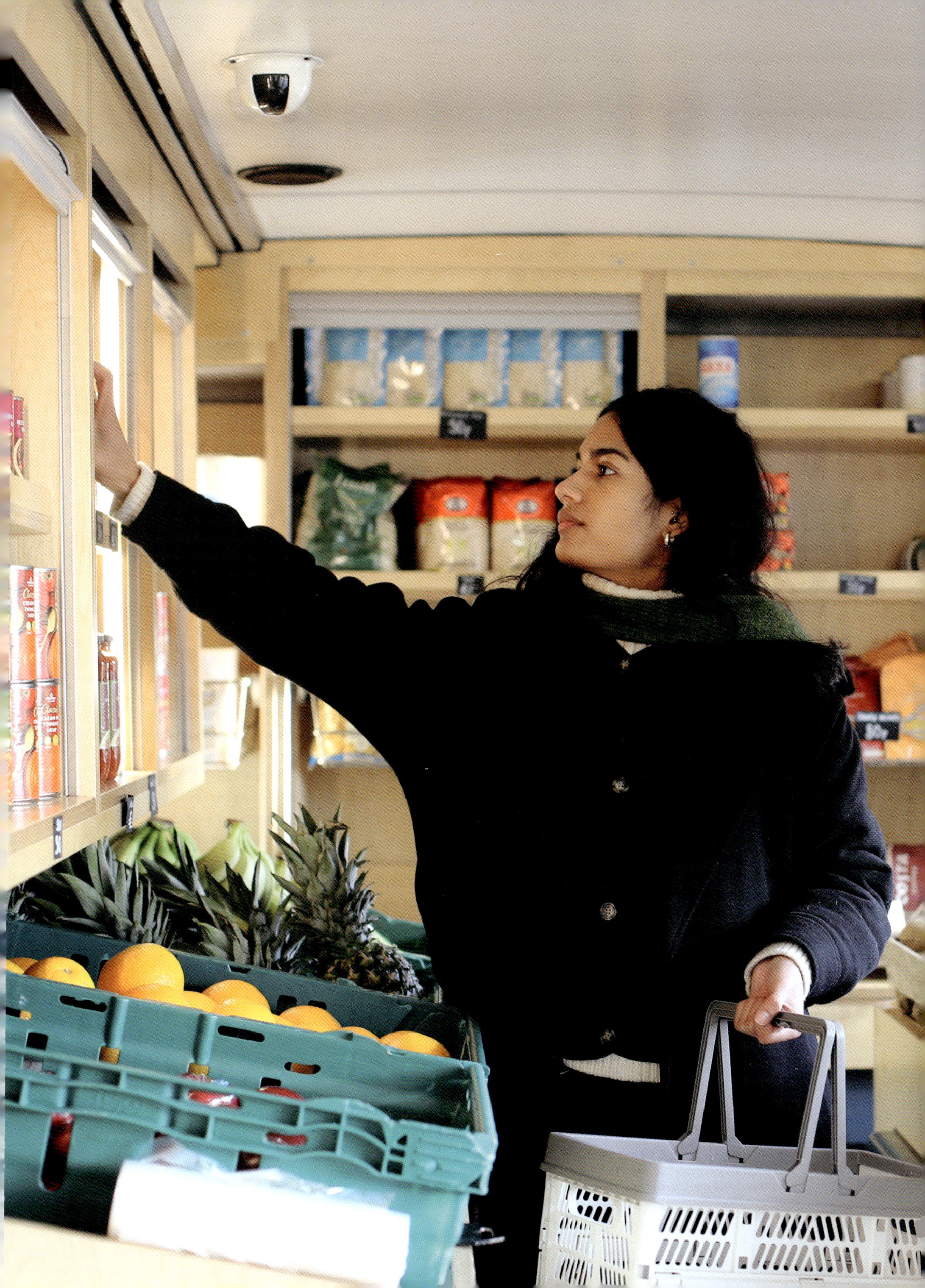

Londoners Making London

JK   KA

Brixton People's Kitchen is a company, it fell on Be Enriched.

Jan: Tell me about how you reach people and what the actual activities are that you are undertaking with the Food Bus.

Kemi: Be Enriched is actually set up to reduce social isolation. We never said that we would actually reduce hunger, because you cannot do that on one meal per week – that's impossible. But we can reduce social isolation, and that should encourage people to go out. And when you go out you are more likely to eat with people and socialise with people and realise that you have some unmet needs as well. That's a very key part for us. The type of people that we target – although our projects are open to everybody – are those most at risk: single-parent families, people affected by ill mental health, disabled people, people with learning disabilities and young people at risk of violence – and adults – and those people recovering from substance misuse. Elderly people are a big percentage of the people that come. We realised that there are about 60 elderly people that come every week and then a mix of around 100 people from those other groups of people. But older people are definitely the largest group that come.

Jan: Food as a social event and food that brings people together rather than just fulfilling a day-to-day need, really.

Kemi: Yes, absolutely. One meal a week does not fulfil your day-to-day needs but if you make a friend you might meet up with them in the week as well, and that's exactly what we try to do with the Food Bus – use it as a focal point for people to meet. I mean, it's been running properly for

4.16 : Kemi working in the kitchen.

Chapter 4 | Temporality + Activation

JK KA

about six months now. It has the cafe on the top deck so people can actually sit and have a conversation. Which people have been doing, especially older women. Indian, Eritrean and Somali women especially.

Jan: So, there was that idea. You told me how the concept for the Food Bus came about. Tell me a little bit about the pragmatics and how you forged the partnership with Feeding Britain and how the funding was then arranged and how the project was delivered.

Kemi: I am from Birmingham. And when I was young there was a man with a van that used to come around our cul-de-sac and everyone would just buy their fruit, veg, whatever off the back of it. No one asked where the food came from, we just ate it. I was very young and that was not really something that I thought about. But it was always that you knew that the food was going to be there on the doorstep at some

4.17 : Sadiq Kahn, Mayor of London, cutting a ribbon to launch the Food Bus.

JK KA

point that week. The shops – I don't actually remember ever going to a supermarket. I remember the man with the van.

Feeding Britain actually contacted us – we were working with the Lambeth Food Partnership, which I am involved in, and I brought up that I'd really like to get a man with a van to get into the places that are food deserts in Lambeth. We had mapped all the food deserts. Real estate is very expensive, but we could get a van to stop somewhere and people to come out and buy their food. And, they mentioned, what about using double-decker buses, because they had had an idea about a bus. And I responded, only as a cafe, because it is very important that we reduce social isolation – it cannot just be food, it has to be somewhere that people can sit down and eat together – and that's literally how it came about. Lambeth did not want the project in the end, so we floated it with the Wandsworth Food Partnership – which is where Be Enriched is based anyway – and everyone really liked the idea. It was very simple, very quick. That's how it came about. Because we are the smaller organisation, we asked them to apply for funding because you are more likely to get it if you have accepted big commissions like that before. We did not know how much it was going to cost.

Jan: What were the challenges along the way? Was there ever a moment where you thought, 'This is never going to happen' Or 'It's not quite turning out the way I was hoping it would.' Was there any doubt along the way?

Kemi: It did take a while to get funding and deliver the project. We had a pandemic in-between.

193

4.18 : Axonometric drawing of the Food Bus. Re-inventing the experience of accessing food aid as a convivial event makes it easier for community members to access wrap-around support.

Chapter 4 | Temporality + Activation

JK   KA

Jan: What were the humps on the road?

    Kemi: We were offered three different buses before we got a bus that worked for us. Then, when we looked into it, it was going to cost us an extra £360k a year if we did not convert the bus so that it was ULEZ [Ultra Low Emission Zone] compliant. Because that legislation changed halfway through the design and the ULEZ circumference in London changed as well. So, we had to make it ULEZ compliant – which is important anyway, because good air quality is important for general health. So that added another £60k I think. The sheer expense of the conversion was a hump, it was shocking.

    I don't think in my mind at any point was it not going to happen. It was a great idea. It was definitely going to happen. We were going to find the money. Feeding Britain were definitely going to make it happen – they are really good partners; they support us monetarily the whole way. Every time it breaks down, we get a bit worried. It has been in the garage since November, so Judy, our bus driver, has been deployed to the kitchen, but as a team we have always been really positive, I think. No matter what happens, we have been very positive, and we want it to succeed. I think that's part of it: having a team that is pushing the whole project forward. It's not just me. Everybody is motivated, and we really love the bus as well, and everyone that uses it really loves it as well. Oh yes, when the bad thing happened, when that person spray-painted the windows and the mirrors for no reason, that was really disheartening actually. That was quite upsetting, that someone from the community who we had designed it for did such a destructive act. That was not good.

JK   KA

Jan: That looked scary, I saw those pictures on Twitter and I thought oh no, this is really needless.

    Kemi: We actually found the person that did it as well. I happen to know a group of graffiti artists, and they said, 'Yes, we know who did it'. I have asked them to meet with us and come and volunteer with us for a day through somebody – I don't know them in person. I would like them to come in and just experience what we do and maybe have a different outlook.

Jan: Thinking about the wider context, you have the Food Bus running, you are still overcoming some operational challenges. Thinking about what your expectations were when the project started and where you are now. Have your expectations been met, exceeded? Would you make fundamentally different decisions along the way if you were to do this again?

    Kemi: Half of me thinks I would maybe not have chosen a double-decker bus to do it on. Another half of me thinks it wouldn't be as good if it were not a double-decker bus – there wouldn't be enough space. I still would like the windows on the side by the kitchen to open, and it would have been good if Covid didn't happen. And if we knew that buses have to be turned over every two weeks so that their engine does not go flat. That's probably it, really.

Jan: In terms of reaching people, are you seeing the engagement that you were hoping for? Are you getting other sorts of people coming around that would not come to events in a food bank or community hall? That are curious? It must be quite novel to drive up in front of someone's house in a food bus?

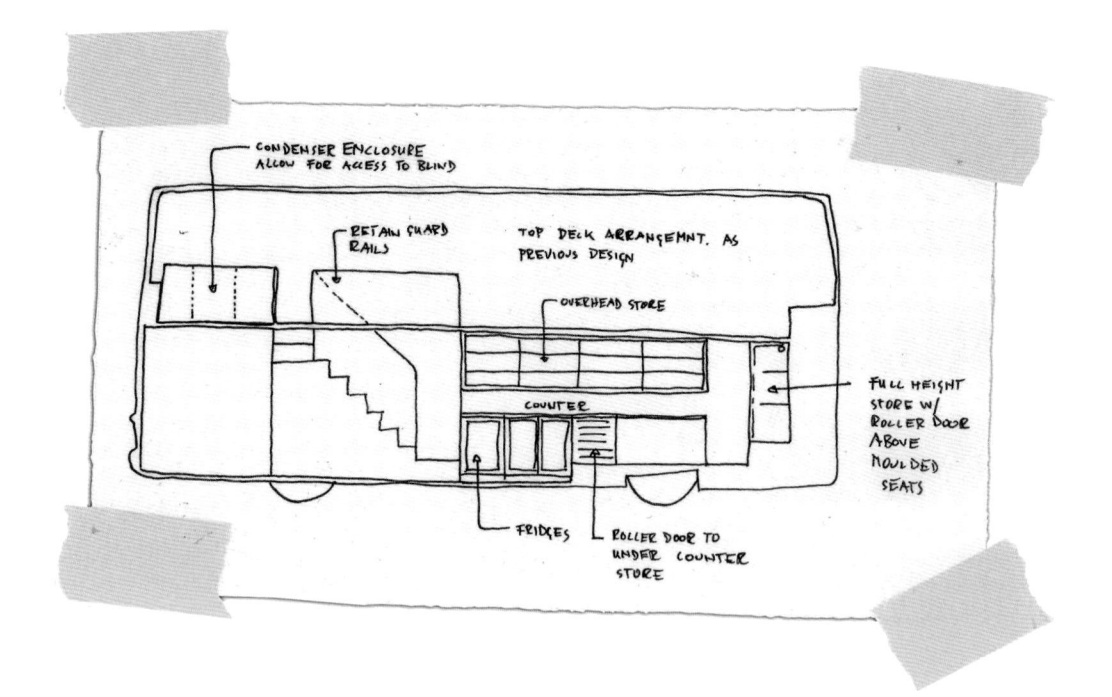

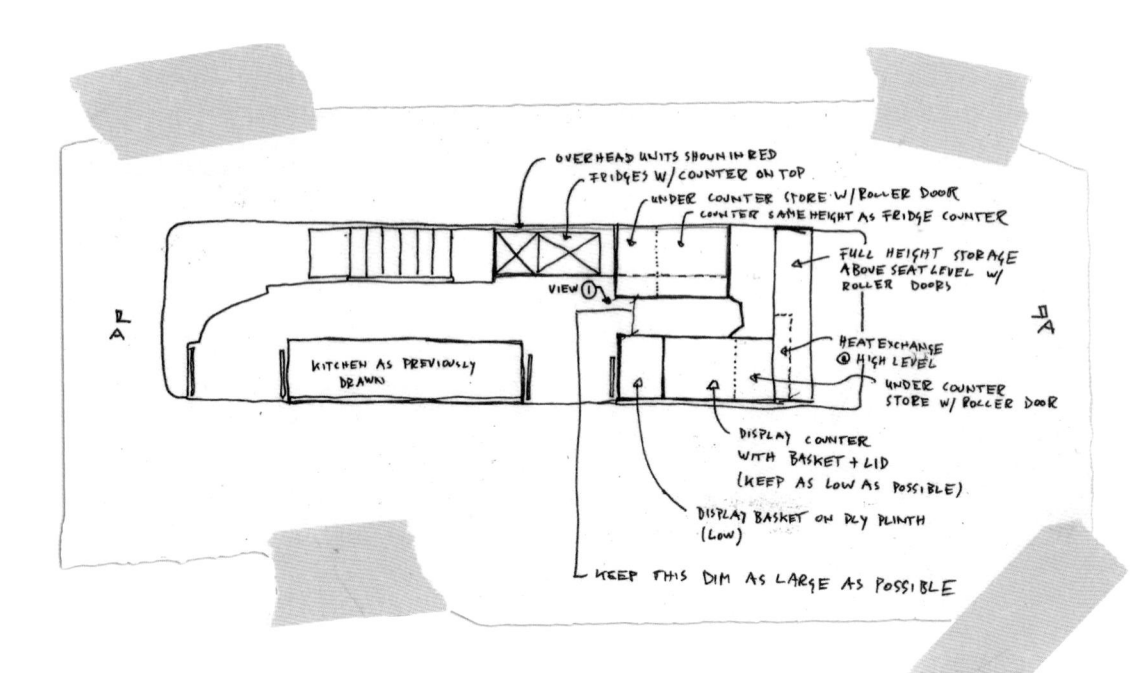

4.19 : Sketches of the Food Bus layout.
4.20 : [ibid]

Chapter 4 | Temporality + Activation

JK   KA

JK   KA

Kemi: Absolutely. We have some quite wealthy people that pop on board – which is great. They come for a bit of novelty. We have also taken, because of Covid and because people don't have inside spaces, we have taken people on their final family trip – how shall I describe it? To commemorate someone that they lost during Covid.

Jan: On the bus?

Kemi: On the bus.

Jan: That's a really big responsibility.

Kemi: Yes, we have done that about three times.

Jan: That's a real honour to be asked for that, because that's quite personal.

Kemi: Yes, so that was something unexpected. We did a food tour and of course the children. I was very much against having children because they are very messy. But kids really love it, and kids

bring their parents, and actually it works in a roundabout way. Kids love getting on the bus and sitting in the front row and pretending to drive and being on the top deck and being able to run about actually. When it's stationary they can run about. It's very novel for them. We have done a couple of school things as well. That's quite nice.

Jan: What precedent do you think the Food Bus has set to support communities and vulnerable individuals?

Kemi: I am really glad we did it, because we have inspired another seven mobile greengrocers across the UK, which is really great. I think the model will be especially useful in rural communities. It's useful for us here in the centre of London. But it will be really good in rural communities and for people who are having trouble going out and getting to the shops where shops are quite far away. Village shops can be quite pricey as well – so maybe a single-level bus would be more useful for rural communities.

What we are doing on the bus is not food aid, it's a more low-cost alternative to the supermarkets. And what we are working on is a food-buying co-operative with other organisations to really drive down the price of food whilst paying a fair price to producers. This sometimes is a complicated balance to juggle because you want to pay enough to farmers so that they are able to live well, but also, we want to provide a price point that people on a low income can actually afford in terms of cost of food. So, we are working on that, and that will be some good learning to share with other people.

4.21 : Elevation of the Food Bus with supergraphic promoting healthy food.

JK　KA

Highlighting the fact that there are no community spaces where people can meet, with youth clubs and community centres all having been converted into luxury flats, having a mobile space is useful. There isn't anywhere that isn't a pub or somewhere you have to pay to go in for local people to socialise. Maybe someone will take that message, and maybe youth and community centres will return. Also, it is providing spaces for people, semi-hard-to-reach young people, older people, people with learning disabilities – it provides opportunities for them to volunteer and get work experience, and volunteering makes people feel useful when they come out and help out on something as novel as a food bus. It's also a bit of a gateway for them to become involved in some of our other Be Enriched activities.

Jan: You grew up in Birmingham you said earlier? What got you here? And what got you interested in this type of work?

Kemi: That's a whole book! Yes, I grew up in Birmingham. We moved to London for better education, when I was six – that's what I think it was, or maybe my mum moved for work, I am not sure. And what got me interested in this type of work is not actually related to me being from Birmingham at all. I was at a bit of a loose end when I was in recovery from a car accident that I had in 2006. I got hit by a car. When I was in recovery and when I was not allowed to work and when I was not allowed to study, I started volunteering with young people in youth offending services. And it was just that, seeing them do the same reparations, painting walls, doing gardening and them telling me when I was mentoring them that they were just learning how to

4.22 : The Food Bus driver.

Chapter 4 | Temporality + Activation

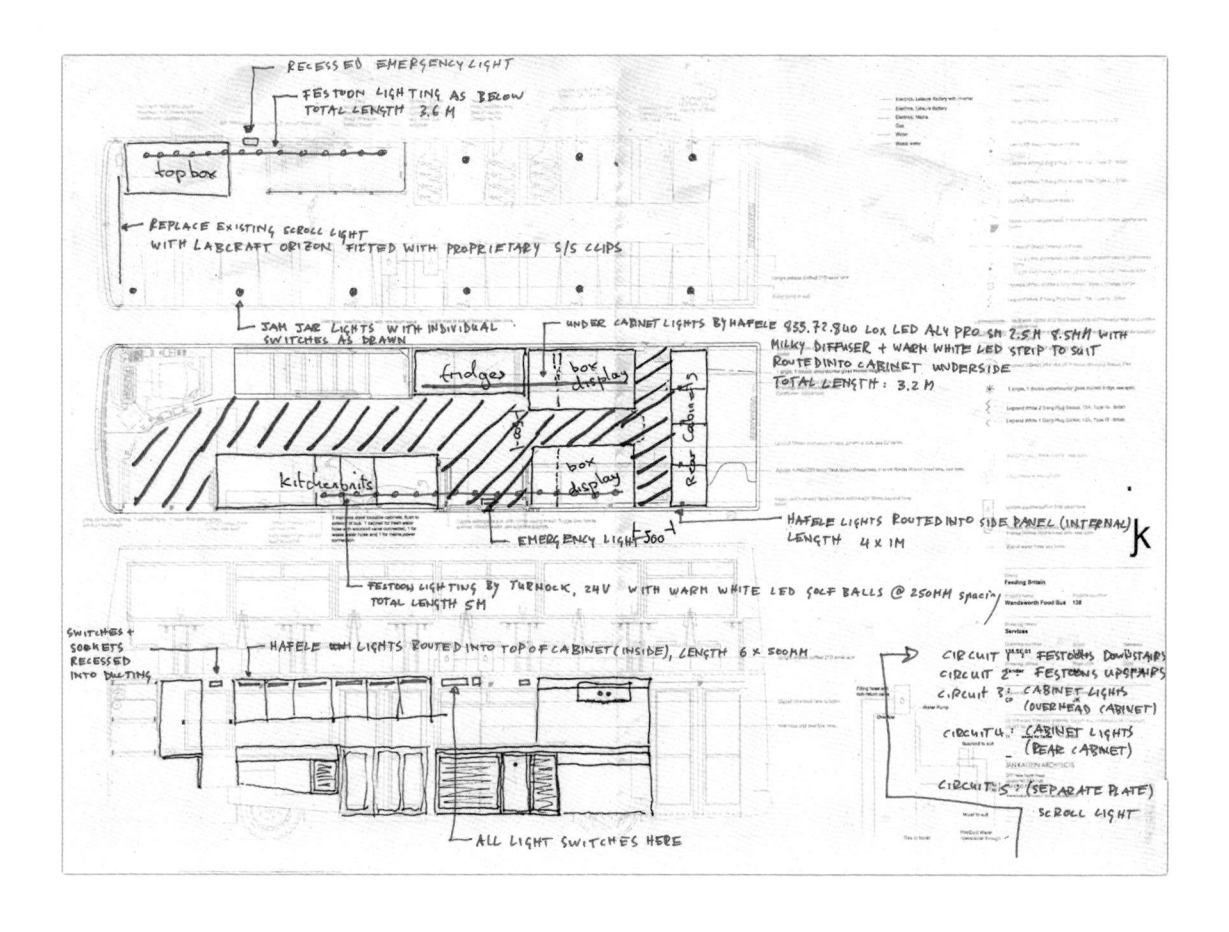

4.23 : Sketches of the Food Bus layout.

4.24 : [next page] Food Bus driver with stocked display shelves. The Food Bus objective is not uniquely to provide handouts, but also to promote healthy eating.

199

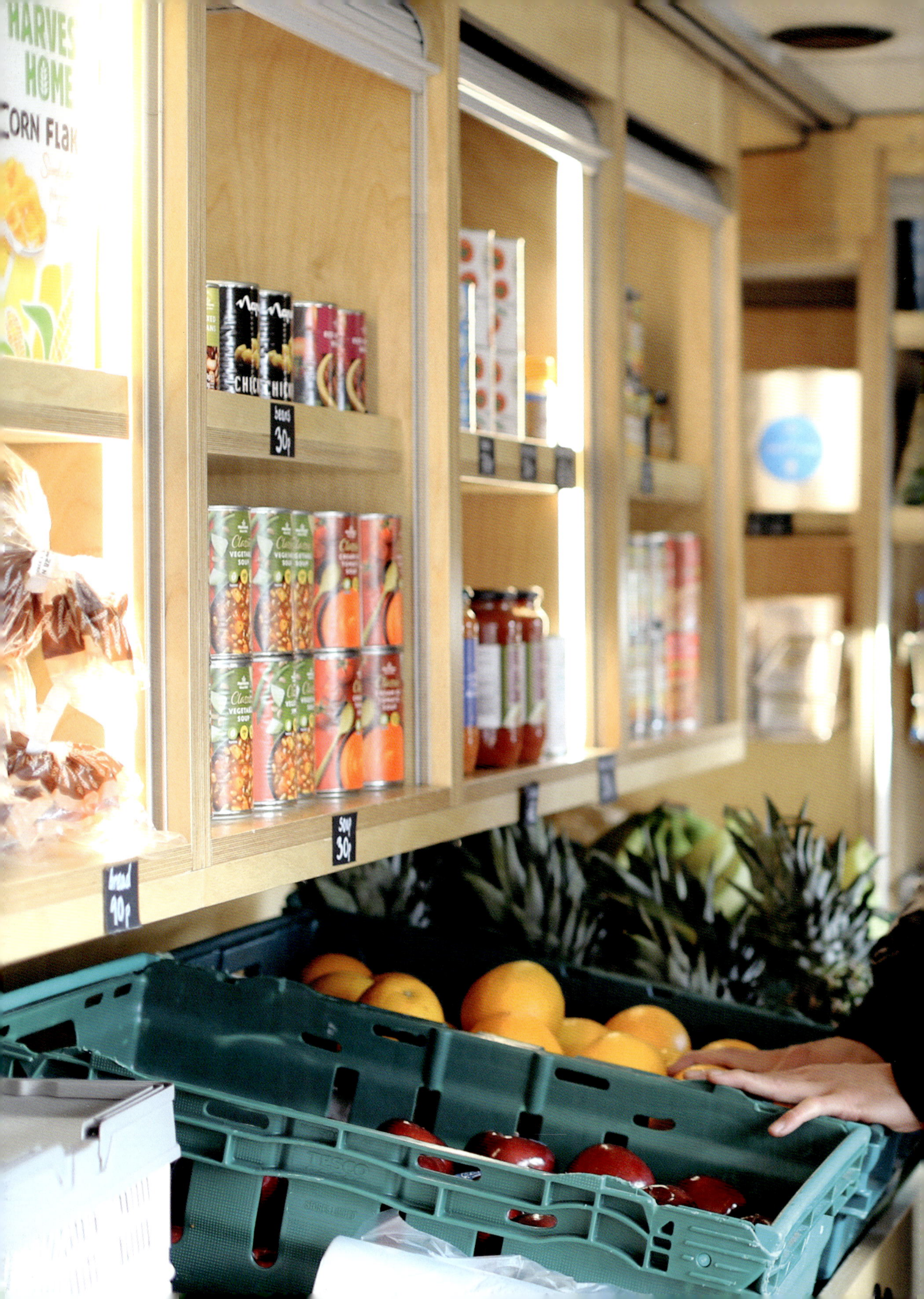
HARVES
HOME
CORN FLAK
beans
30p
Soup
30p
bread
90p

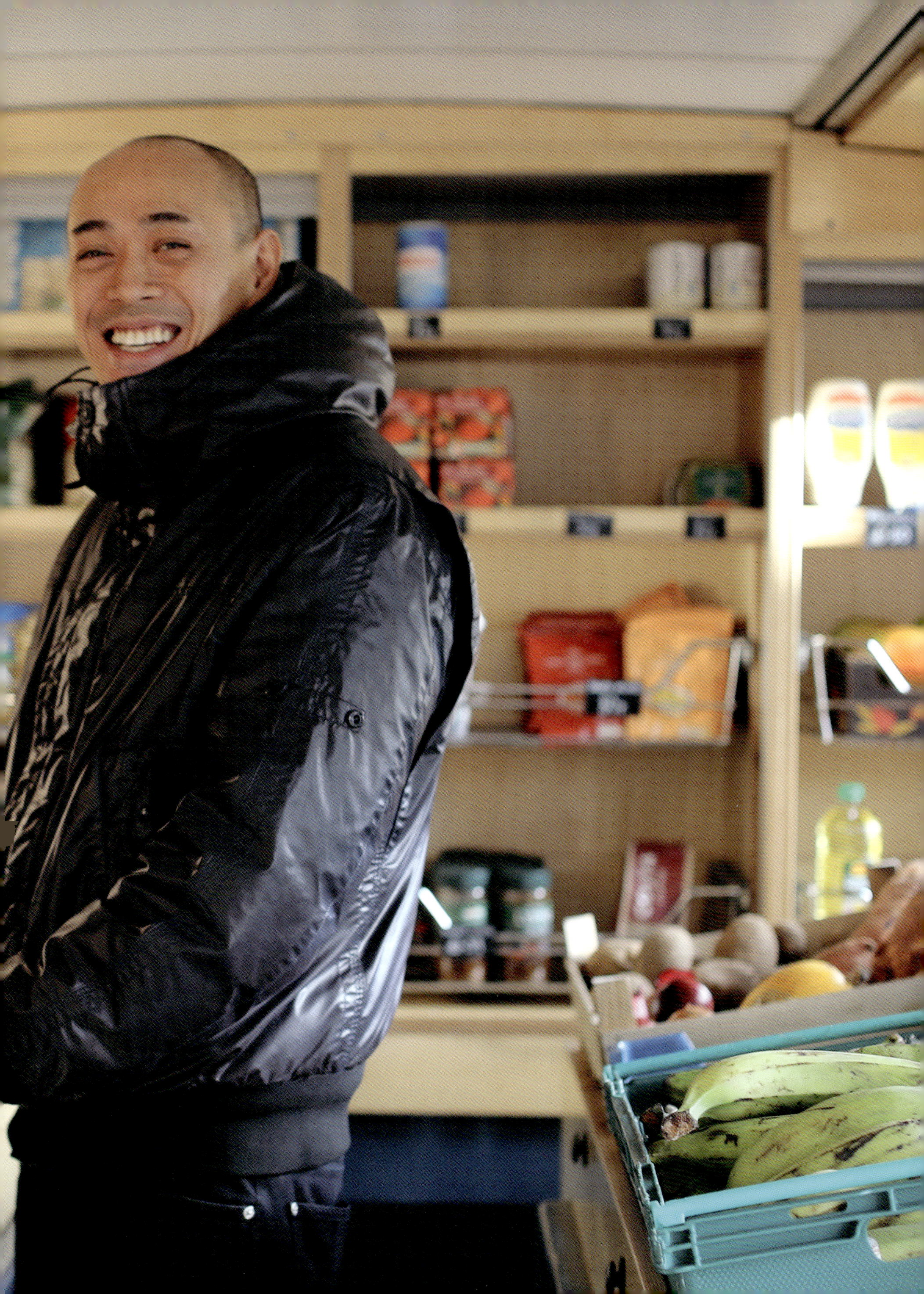

4.25 : Back entrance of the Food Bus.

Chapter 4 | Temporality + Activation

JK   KA

KA do crimes a lot better than when they did it and they got caught. That made me think that they should maybe just be involved in doing something totally different. And that was when my friend said, 'What about using all this food to bring people together?' And I thought that would be a really good opportunity. And I did that for a few years. And then I went to work for a charity working with young people. And then I did a degree – sorry, I retrained: my first degree is in architecture. And my second degree is in youth and community work. And then I started to pay more attention to the social aspects of the community meals. And I did an MA in psychology and focused on food psychology and found how that can really change people's behaviour, health-wise-, but also social-wise. Then I started researching the reasons that people were actually coming to my meals and realised that they were not coming for food, actually; they were coming to meet other people, and that's the main reason they come. They said in the survey, it was number 1 they came to socialise and meet a friend, and number 2 they really enjoy the staff there and number 3 they come for the food. And our food is amazing, but still, that's not the real reason that people come.

Jan: Thank you, Kemi.

4.26 : The upper deck is designed for social interaction and exchange and to host events and workshops around food and well-being.
4.27 : Detail of upper deck table with jam jar light.

203

Creativity, Authorship + Governance

Creativity, Charles Landry writes in his book *The Creative City*, is often exclusively associated with the arts. In the context of finance and management, terms such as 'creative accounting' suggest a derogatory connotation, referencing inaccurate or even irregular practice. Yet, Landry continues, cities thrive because of their social and political creativity. Cities 'have one crucial resource – their people. Human cleverness, desires, motivations, imagination, and creativity are replacing location, natural resources and market access.' London's success depends on the creative capital of those who design and operate systems of governance, service and care.

London has always had the capacity to attract some of the best and brightest talent. Those who have come to London with limited means have learned to improvise amidst high rents and coarse-meshed social security, and those who have stayed to establish a family have had to contend with some of the highest childcare costs in Europe. Londoners have had to become resilient and creative. Their creativity is not only vested in arts and culture, but there are also examples across all kinds of personal and professional lives, including the nine recounted in this book.

I was aware of the incredible work that my interviewees were doing when I started writing this book. I knew about the importance of organisation, determination, agency and collaboration. What I did not expect is the significance of what several of my interviewees describe as 'the crack in the system'. The crack in the system is the necessary imperfection in established policy, process and governance that makes space for creativity.

In the UK, the capacity of communities to look after each other during the pandemic stood in stark contrast to the government's largely ineffective response, aspects of which were recently found to be unlawful. The policy position on climate change is weakened by economic interests and is by many seen as not adequately responding to the urgency of the challenges at hand.

How might one design a governance model that intentionally includes cracks to invite a creative response with more immediate and equitable benefits for communities? What might we learn from London to equip the public with the tools and resources to design simpler and yet more profound solutions? And how can these cracks be designed to create opportunity whilst preventing exploitation and abuse?

Nabeel Hamdi's book *Small Change: About the Art of Practice and the Limits of Planning in Cities* recounts the story of the relocation of a bus stop from a major expressway to the centre of a favela, and the consequential flourishing of economic and social activity around the new bus stop. Moving a bus stop involves the replanning of the bus route and subsequently the physical relocation of the pole and flag. The work will be undertaken by a transit planner and a municipal works department, professions not usually associated with creative practice. Yet, the story represents a simple and effective example of a methodology that relies on an intimate understanding of local parameters to enable wide-ranging change through a small but unequivocal act of creativity.

The Creative Bureaucracy Festival held annually in Berlin builds on Landry's premise to celebrate innovation at all levels of government, bringing together those who are fighting 'for the common good and make a difference'. The festival has a dual purpose, propagating recognition of public sector 'bureaucrats' and shifting the perception of the sector from a service provider to creative innovator. Whilst the festival represents a timely recognition of the creative capacity of governments and public administration, it fails to recognise those without administrative duty or professional appointment who are increasingly driving change in cities.

London has developed its very own response. Eva Sørensen describes the concept of 'loose governance'. This is not to be confused with the neo-liberal agenda of a diminished government. 'Liberty', she writes, 'is a way of governing and not an opposing concept.' In other words, good governance does not abolish government, but it shifts its remit to enable participation and empowerment.

My colleagues at Jan Kattein Architects have been involved in the implementation of several of the projects described in this book. What has been fundamental to their success is a careful evaluation of our role as practitioners. My book, *The Architecture Chronicle: Diary of an Architectural Practice*, establishes a framework for this, identifying three characters that are united in contemporary architectural practice. The book describes the architect-inventor, the architect-activist and the architect-arbitrator. The success of our work relies on a skilled balancing act between these three characters. The parameters that define each project are different, and there are varying requirements from project stage to project stage. However, what is consistent across our work is a renewed understanding of authorship. In all these projects, the creative act is the result of a common effort across disciplines and in collaboration with stakeholders. We largely enable such genuine collaboration despite governmental and professional process – rather than because of it.

Jonathan Hill draws parallels between Roland Barthes's theory of 'The Death of the Author' and his own understanding of architecture. Where for Barthes literature emerges in the creative space between the author and the reader, for Hill architecture materialises between the building and its user. The reader according to Barthes or the user according to Hill is contributor to the creative act through which literature or architecture is made. The author or the architect are overrated in the creation of literature or architecture. Applying the same mantra to our discussion in this book, one might say that London is a product of its buildings, streets, squares and gardens, and inhabitants. Given that the term 'architect' has legal protection in the UK, the necessary contribution of the user to the creation of architecture in Hill's theory engenders the 'Illegal Architect', the creator of architecture not permitted to use the title 'architect'.

Barthes's contemporary, Guy Debord, with his psycho-geographic maps titled 'The Naked City', goes one step further to ascribe authorship of urban space exclusively to those who experience it. The buildings, streets, squares and gardens of the city are a naked backdrop to the creative act which takes place in the mind of the beholder. 'The Naked City' declares the death of the urbanist, planner or architect.

Why, despite the lack of credit that communities have been given to date for their creative contribution to the city, is bottom-up urbanism thriving in London? I have found four principal reasons why communities are increasingly driving change.

Firstly, neo-liberal agendas promoted by government, including Brexit, have drained local administrations of resources, in particular in London, incapacitating them from implementing transformational change at pace. Secondly, emergent challenges including the recent pandemic require urgent and granular responses which large organisations, including public administrations, are struggling to deliver. Thirdly, community organisations are well placed to implement incremental change, which is increasingly seen as a way of driving innovation and mitigating political polarisation. And finally, it is becoming apparent that economic growth, which has for decades been seen as the primary means by which to reverse poverty, is in fact exacerbating the problem, furthering both environmental collapse and inequality.

My interviewees are motivated by their desire to respond to apparent deficiencies, whether this is the critique of an unjust food system, a car-dominated city, the lack of ecological leadership or unethical business practice. Their response is through direct action. A government response occurs through policy. The former is immediate yet constrained in scale. The latter is slow, yet all-encompassing. Direct action relies on learning by doing, whereas policymaking relies on prediction and forecasting. Both are a form of democratic governance, direct action because it relies on mobilising others to its cause, policymaking because it draws its authority from debate, iterative refinement and ultimately a majority vote.

Good governance needs both, direct action to address granular, local challenges, build community, drive innovation and develop and test new concepts, and policymaking, to deliver change at scale, set targets and monitor impact. Direct action alone lacks the reflective power of policymaking, and policymaking lacks the imminent applicability and capacity building inherent in direct action. Both processes stand in competition, with policy seeking to regulate action and action inhabiting the cracks in policy.

In London we are at the dawn of a new type of bureaucracy relying on a symbiosis between loose governance and direct action. Loose governance is providing the reflective and analytical component of policymaking. Direct action is delivering innovation and proof of concept. Both together build consensus, capacity and community. To close the circle, we must weigh forbearance and planning equally with direct action and subsequent post-rationalisation.

The role of the professional in this scenario shifts from being the author of ideas to enabling the creativity of others.

About the Author /

Jan Kattein, DipArch, MArch, PhD, FIPM, is an author, lecturer and practitioner who lives in London. After completing a degree, postgraduate diploma and master's in architecture at The Bartlett, he worked in social housing before pursuing a brief career in theatre design. In 2004 he finally established his own studio, Jan Kattein Architects.

Jan's PhD thesis, *The Architecture Chronicle: Diary of an Architectural Practice*, which was published as a book by Ashgate, provided a platform for him to critically reflect on the role of the architect and cement his interest in open and inclusive forms of design practice. His research has established the methodology that characterises his studio's work today.

He is lecturer in Architecture and Engagement at The Bartlett, University College London, a fellow of the Institute of Place Management at the Manchester Metropolitan University Business School and a registered architect in the UK and the Netherlands. His contribution transcends disciplinary boundaries and includes writing, speaking, architecture, design and urbanism.

Today, Jan Kattein Architects is recognised internationally as one of the leading placemaking and participatory design practices, with award-winning projects that are celebrated for their spatial and civic accomplishments.

BIBLIOGRAPHY

Adelman, Clem (1993), 'Kurt Lewin and the Origins of Action Research', *Educational Action Research*, 1:1, pp 7–24, https://www.tandfonline.com/doi/abs/10.1080/0965079930010102

Bishop, Peter, and Williams, Lesley (2012), *The Temporary City*, London and New York: Routledge

Broome, Jon (1986), 'The Segal Method', *The Architects' Journal*, Special Issue, pp 31–68.

Casas-Valle, Daniel (2022), 'The Future Design of Streets', Presentation at Placemaking Week Europe, 27–30 September 2022, Pontevedra, Spain

Creative Bureaucracy Festival, https://creativebureaucracy.org/

Department for Digital, Culture, Media and Sport (2021), Community Life Survey 2020/21, https://www.gov.uk/government/statistics/community-life-survey-202021

Gayle, Damien (2022), 'People of Colour Far Likelier to Live in England's Very High Air Pollution Areas', *The Guardian*, 4 October 2022, https://www.theguardian.com/environment/2022/oct/04/people-of-colour-likelier-live-england-very-high-air-pollution-areas

Hamdi, Nabeel (2004), *Small Change, About the Art of Practice and the Limits of Planning in Cities*, London and Sterling, VA: Earthscan

Hill, Jonathan (1998), *The Illegal Architect*, London: Black Dog Publishing

Jacobs, Jane (1961), *The Death and Life of Great American Cities*, New York: Random House

Kattein, Jan (2014), *The Architecture Chronicle: Diary of an Architectural Practice*, Farnham, Surrey: Ashgate

Landry, Charles (1995), *The Creative City*, London: Demos

Landry, Charles (2006), The Art of City Making, London and Sterling, VA: Earthscan

Landry, Charles, https://archive.charleslandry.com/panel/themes/making-great-cities/

Mazzucato, Mariana, and Collington, Rosie (2023), *The Big Con: How the Consulting Industry Weakens Our Businesses, Infantilizes Our Governments and Warps Our Economies*, London: Penguin Books

Moos, David, and Trechsel, Gail (eds) (2003), *Samuel Mockbee and the Rural Studio: Community Architecture*, Birmingham, AL: Birmingham Museum of Art

Quality of Life Foundation (2022), Your Quality of Life Community Report, https://hggt.co.uk/wp-content/uploads/2023/01/QOLF-Community-Feedback-Report_151222-FINAL.pdf

Quinn, Daniel (1999), *Beyond Civilization: Humanity's Next Great Adventure*, New York: Harmony Books (with Richard Buckminster Fuller quote on p.137)

Riddiford, Jane (2021), *Learning to Lead Together – An Ecological and Community Approach*, Abingdon, Oxfordshire: Routledge

Sennett, Richard (2009), *The Craftsman*, London: Penguin Books

Sørensen, Eva (2002), 'Democratic Theory and Network Governance', *Administrative Theory and Praxis*, 24:4, pp 693–720, https://www.

tandfonline.com/doi/abs/10.1080/10841806.2002.11029383

Steel, Carolyn (2008), *Hungry City: How Food Shapes Our Lives,* London: Vintage/Random House

United Nations, Sustainable Development Goals, https://www.un.org/sustainabledevelopment/sustainable-development-goals/

Warshafsky, Gabriel, 'We Build Community Through Design', https://jankattein.com/

IMAGE CREDITS

1.01 : *Jan Kattein Architects*
1.02 : *Jon Sturrock*
1.03 : *Jon Sturrock*
1.04 : *Jon Sturrock*
1.05 : *Jan Kattein Architects*
1.06 : *Jan Kattein Architects*
1.07 : *Jan Kattein Architects*
1.08 : *Jan Kattein Architects*
1.09 : *Jan Kattein Architects*
1.10 : *Jan Kattein Architects*
1.11 : *Jan Kattein Architects*
1.12 : *Jan Kattein Architects*
1.13 : *Jan Kattein Architects*
1.14 : *Jan Kattein Architects*
1.15 : *Jan Kattein Architects*
1.16 : *Yangyang Liu*
1.17 : *Jan Kattein Architects*
1.18 : *Jan Kattein Architects*
1.19 : *Jan Kattein Architects*
1.20 : *Jan Kattein Architects*
1.21 : *Jan Kattein Architects*
1.22 : *Jan Kattein Architects*
1.23 : *Jan Kattein Architects*
1.24 : *Jan Kattein Architects*
1.25 : *Jan Kattein Architects*
1.26 : *Andy Bailey*
1.27 : *Jan Kattein Architects*
1.28 : *Chloë Dunnett*
1.29 : *Lara Arnott*
1.30 : *Rachel Jones*
1.31 : *Andy Bailey*
1.32 : *Andy Bailey*
1.33 : *Andrew Porter Photography*
1.34 : *Andrew Porter Photography*
1.35 : *Lara Arnott*
1.36 : *Andrew Porter Photography*

1.37 : *Chloë Dunnett*

2.01 : *Jan Kattein Architects*
2.02 : *Jan Kattein Architects*
2.03 : *Jan Kattein Architects*
2.04 : *Jan Kattein Architects*
2.05 : *Jan Kattein Architects*
2.06 : *Jan Kattein Architects*
2.07 : *Jan Kattein Architects*
2.08 : *Jan Kattein Architects*
2.09 : *Jan Kattein Architects*
2.10 : *Jan Kattein Architects*
2.11 : *Jan Kattein Architects*
2.12 : *Rachel Kitchen*
2.13 : *Jan Kattein Architects*
2.14 : *Jan Kattein Architects*
2.15 : *Jan Kattein Architects*
2.16 : *Jan Kattein Architects*
2.17 : *Jan Kattein Architects*
2.18 : *Jan Kattein Architects*
2.19 : *Jan Kattein Architects*
2.20 : *Jan Kattein Architects*
2.21 : *Jan Kattein Architects*
2.22 : *Jan Kattein Architects*
2.23 : *Jan Kattein Architects*
2.24 : *FEL*
2.25 : *Jan Kattein Architects*
2.26 : *Jan Kattein Architects*
2.27 : *FEL*
2.28 : *FEL*
2.29 : *Jan Kattein Architects*
2.30 : *Jan Kattein Architects*
2.31 : *FEL*
2.32 : *Ella Stoneham-Bull*
2.33 : *Jan Kattein Architects*
2.34 : *RUSS*
2.35 : *Jan Kattein Architects*
2.36 : *Ella Stoneham-Bull*
2.37 : *Ella Stoneham-Bull*
2.38 : *Ella Stoneham-Bull*

3.01 : *Jan Kattein Architects*
3.02 : *www.warrencooperphotography-corporate.com*
3.03 : *Jan Kattein Architects*
3.04 : *Jan Kattein Architects*
3.05 : *Jan Kattein Architects*
3.06 : *Jan Kattein Architects*
3.07 : *Jan Kattein Architects*
3.08 : *www.warrencooperphotography-corporate.com*
3.09 : *Jan Kattein Architects*
3.10 : *Jan Kattein Architects*
3.11 : *Jan Kattein Architects*
3.12 : *Jan Kattein Architects*
3.13 : *Jan Kattein Architects*
3.14 : *Jan Kattein Architects*
3.15 : *Jan Kattein Architects*
3.16 : *www.warrencooperphotography-corporate.com*
3.17 : *www.warrencooperphotography-corporate.com*
3.18 : *www.warrencooperphotography-corporate.com*
3.19 : *Jan Kattein Architects*
3.20 : *Jan Kattein Architects*
3.21 : *Jan Kattein Architects*
3.22 : *ACAVA*
3.23 : *Jan Kattein Architects*
3.24 : *ACAVA*
3.25 : *ACAVA*
3.26 : *ACAVA*
3.27 : *ACAVA*
3.28 : *ACAVA*
3.29 : *ACAVA*
3.30 : *ACAVA*

4.01 : *photo: Hassan Hajjaj, styling: Samson Soboye*
4.02 : *Morley Van Sternberg*
4.03 : *Molax productions*
4.04 : *Hassan Hajjaj*
4.05 : *photo: Hassan Hajjaj, styling: Samson Soboye*
4.06 : *photo: Hassan Hajjaj, styling: Samson Soboye*
4.07 : *photo: Hassan Hajjaj, styling: Samson Soboye*
4.08 : *Molax productions*
4.09 : *Molax productions*
4.10 : *Molax productions*
4.11 : *Molax productions*
4.12 : *Hassan Hajjaj*
4.13 : *Anna Mill*
4.14 : *Jan Kattein Architects*
4.15 : *Jan Kattein Architects*
4.16 : *Jan Kattein Architects*
4.17 : *Jan Kattein Architects*
4.18 : *Jan Kattein Architects*
4.19 : *Jan Kattein Architects*
4.20 : *Jan Kattein Architects*
4.21 : *Jan Kattein Architects*
4.22 : *Jan Kattein Architects*
4.23 : *Jan Kattein Architects*
4.24 : *Jan Kattein Architects*
4.25 : *Jan Kattein Architects*
4.26 : *Jan Kattein Architects*
4.27 : *Jan Kattein Architects*

INDEX

Note: italic page numbers indicate figures, and captions to figures.

ACAVA (Association for Cultural Advancement through Visual Art) 154, 155, 160
action research 19, 22
    activation 168
activism 11, 19, 27, 32, 35, 121, 176
    direct action 50, 55, 207
African Street Style (Hackney) 12, 15, 170–187, *174–5, 177, 185*
    and activism/politics 176, 184–7
    and African diaspora 172, 181
    Calvert Avenue/Boundary Estate location of 172, 173–6
    challenges with 179–81
    and community engagement 172, 173, 178
    and ownership of public space 176, 179, *182, 183*
    photography studio at *171,* 176, 178, *178, 179, 180,* 181, *184*
    temporality/informality of 169, 178
Akinola, Kemi 168, 169, 190–192, *191, 192,* 193, 198–203
    see also Food Bus
ASOS 96, 98, 102, 108
Auckland (New Zealand) 19, 22, 38
authorship 11, 206

Be Enriched 168, 191–2, 193, 198
biodiversity 19, 35, 50, 52, *55,* 57
Blue House Yard (Wood Green) 70–71, 128, 130–151, *131, 134, 135, 136–7, 138, 139*
    and apprentices 138, *142–3,* 150
    bus café at 141, *144, 150, 151*
    civic space in 132, *146–7*
    and community engagement 135–8, 141–5, 150
    crises in construction of 138–140
    lessons from 141, 148–150
    maintenance of workshops 144, *145*
    occupants of *148, 149,* 150
    as temporary 132, 168
    and volunteers 132, 140, *141*
Bohill, Emily 70, 74, 75–6, *75,* 79, 80, 88–9
    see also Thornhill Library
Boundary Estate (Tower Hamlets) 172, 173–6, 179
Brexit 66, 101–2, 207
British Library 22, 42–7, *46–7,* 47
Brixton People's Kitchen 190, 191, 192
Broome, Jon 70, 114, 115–17, *115,* 118–21, *120,* 122, 123, 125

Camden 25, 30, 38, 84
charities 27, 47, 74, 114, 190, 203
children 23, *24,* 25–7, 63, 197
    see also Thornhill Library
Church Grove (Lewisham) 70, 112–25
    and community 115, 116, 118, 119–120, 121, 123, 125
    and Community Land Trust 114, 118, 120
    and competitive tender 116–17
    and contractor/self-builder liability *124–5*
    and funding 118, 121, 122
    and Greater London Authority 105, 117, 121, 122
    and housing development process 117–18
    and housing mix 119
    lessons from 123–5
    and Lewisham Council 116, 117, 118, 119, 121
    and over-budget crisis 121–3
    and resale terms 120
    and RUSS organisational structure 118, 121
    self-builders at *113,* 119, *122–3*
    and sustainable neighbourhood concept 116, 118–19, 120, 123
    and volunteers 117, 118, 119
climate change 15, 19, 50, 57, 114, 204
clothing industry *see* Fashion Enter Ltd
collaborative approach 11, 14, 15, 19, 47, 128, 132, 205
    see also under Skip Garden
communities and planning 11, 14–15
communities and self-build housing 115, 116, 118, 119–120, 121, 123, 125, 128
community engagement/cohesion 13, 14, 22, 50, 129, 141–8, 172, 173, 190, 191, 195–7, 205
community gardens 61, 66, 116, 145, 148
Community Land Trust 114, 118, 120
community-building 19, 23, *33,* 47
Covid 19 pandemic 50, 52, 109, 191, 193, 195, 197,

204, 206
creativity 12, 13, 70, 155, 159–160, 172, 184, 204, 205–6

Dayes, Kareem 115, 116, 119
direct action 50, 55, 206
Dunnett, Chloë 12, 19, 50–52, *51*
   see also Sitopia Farm

ecology 11, 14, 19, 22, 23–5
education
   architectural *34,* 128, 133, 135
   and community-led housing 114, 115
   environmental/ecological 14, 22, 25–7, 62
   and manufacturing *95, 100,* 101, 102–5
   and project development 70
   see also Thornhill Library
El-Sady, Rasha 12, 128–9, 154, *155,* 159
   see also Maxilla Men's Shed
entrepreneurship 61, 62, 101, 128, 141, *148,* 151
ethical/unethical practices 70, 97, 98, 101, 206
Evaporation Coolstore, Skip Garden (Conning-Rowland) *28–9, 30, 31, 42*

Fashion Enter Ltd 71, 96, 97–101
   see also Tailoring Academy
Feeding Britain 193, 195
food banks 52, 169, *189,* 191
Food Bus 188–203, *194,* 195, *197, 198, 200–201, 202*
   and children 197
   and community engagement/cohesion 190, 191, 195–7, 203
   conversion costs for 195
   and Covid 191, 193, 195, 197
   layout of *189,* 190, *196, 199*
   partnerships with charities 190, 191–2, 193, 195
   and social isolation 191, 192, 193
   target users of 192, 198
   temporality/informality of 168, 169
   upper deck as mobile community space 191, 198, *201*
   vandalising of 195
food policy 51, 55, 66

food poverty 50, 53, 169, 190
food production 12, 14, 19, 25, 50, 51, 52
   community gardens 61, 66, 116, 145, 148
   and land use/ownership 50, 52, 53, 62, 66
   sustainable 53, 114, 115
   see also Sitopia Farm
food systems 50, 51, 52, 53, 55, 57, 61, 62–3, 206

Galaxius (performance-related pay system) 101
gardens 11, 19, 35
   community 61, 66, 116, 123, 145, 148
   educational ecology 14, 22, 25–7
   see also Skip Garden
Glass House Lantern, Skip Garden (Taylor) *21, 25, 28–9, 39, 42*
Global Generation 14, 19, 22, 23, 27, 32–8, 44
   approach to communities of 27–30
   and Story Garden 22, 42–7, *46–7*
Greater London Authority 13–14, 105, 117, 121, 122
Greenwich *see* Sitopia Farm
Greenwich Co-operative Development Agency 52

Hackney 51, 52, 81
   see also African Street Style
Hadzhalie, Iman Mohd *26*
Hardy, Alice 128, 132–8, *133,* 140
   see also Blue House Yard
Harringay *see* Tailoring Academy
Holloway, Jane 96–8, *97*
   see also Tailoring Academy
housing
   affordable 70, 119, 120
   community-led *see* RUSS
   development 117–18, 128
   social 120, 123, 128

immigration 12, 98–9
inequality 15, 19, 74, 76, 206
Islington 74, 76, 79, 96, 105
   see also Thornhill Library

Jan Kattein Architects 11, 132, 205

Kensington *see* Maxilla Men's Shed
King, Julia 22, 38, 128
King's Cross 14, 25, 35
    see also Skip Garden

Landry, Charles 70, 204, 205
leadership 11, 19, 22
learning by doing 117, 132, 135, 206
Lennon, Jeffrey 12, 15, 168, 172–3, *173*, 181–4
    see also African Street Style
Lewisham *see* Church Grove
Little Free Libraries 76, 78–9
Liu, Yangyang *36–7*
local authorities 13, 15, 116, 145, 179, 187
London/Londoners 12–14, 15
    and creativity 12, 205, 206–7
    governance structure of 13–14, 205
    Mayor of 13, 15, 52, 57, *193*
London Olympics (2012) 172, 173, 185

Maxilla Men's Shed (North Kensington) 12, 152–65, *156*
    and ACAVA 154, 155, 160
    activities offered at *153*, 155, *158*
    and communities 157–160, 161, 164
    and creativity 155, 159, 160
    lessons from 161–4
    and Men's Shed movement 154, 155, 159
    participants at 155, 157, *157*
    sharing/acquiring skills at 154, 155, 157, *165*
    socialising at 128–9, 154, 155, 160–161, *161, 162–3*
Meanwhile Space (social enterprise) 70–71, 132
Men's Shed movement 59, 154, 155
mentoring 71, 102–5, 198–203
Michaelides, Jo 74, 75

neighbourhood transformation 11, 14
    and sustainability 116, 118–19, 123
networks 13, 14, 84, 98, 159
New Zealand 19, 22, 23, 27, 38, 42, 47

obesity epidemic 50, 53, 66
organic farming/gardening 12, 25, 50
    see also Sitopia Farm; Skip Garden

Paper Garden (Canada Water) 22, 44
Pertwood (Wiltshire) 25–7, 32
printing technology 105–8
problem-solving 13, 157, 164
public spaces 13, 14, 168, 169, 179, 184, 185

recycling/upcycling *30–31*, 35, 42, 105
Redman, Charlie *40–41*
reflexive city 70
Riddiford, Jane 19, 22, *23*
    see also Skip Garden
Rise Phoenix 25, 32
risk aversion 70, 109, 121
road network 13, 168, 169, 179
Run Kids Run 71, 74, 84
Run Thornhill Run 80, 81–4, *88*
Rural Studio (Alabama, US) 128
RUSS (Rural Urban Synthesis Society) 71, 114–17, *117*
    self-build project of *see* Church Grove

Segal, Walter/Segal Method 114, 116, 128
self-build projects *see* Blue House Yard; Church Grove
Sitopia Farm (Greenwich) 12, 19, 48–67, *56, 63, 66–7*
    and biodiversity 50, 52, 55, 57
    business model of 50, 57–61
    dining event at 57, *58–9*
    and direct action/advocacy for change 50, 55–7, 61–2
    flower production at *54, 57, 64*
    and food poverty 50, 53
    and obesity epidemic 50, 53, 66
    organic ethos of 53–7
    and production–consumption connection 50, *60*, 62–6
    and volunteers 50, 52, *53*, 61, 62
    and Woodlands Farm Trust 52–3, 61
Skip Garden (King's Cross) 14, 19, 20–47, *24, 25, 28–9, 42*
    chicken coop (Vyvial) *35, 44, 45*
    and collaborative approach 22, 27–32, *32, 34, 36–7*, 38, 128
    and community-building 19, 23, *33*
    Evaporation Coolstore *see* Evaporation Coolstore

funding for 38
Glass House Lantern *see* Glass House Lantern
Hall of 100 Hands *28–9*
legacy of 14, 38, *46–7*
Lunch and Learning event at *33,* 38
and storytelling 22, 23, 38–42, 47
as temporary 38, 168
Vertical Living Landscape (Hadzhalie) 26
Welcome Shelter (Redman) *40–41*
Slotover, Kate 74, 75, *75,* 76–8, 79–81, 84–8
see also Thornhill Library
Soboye, Samson 176, 181
social enterprise 50, 52, 70–71, 96, 109
social housing 120, 123, 128
social isolation 128–9, 155, 160, 191, 192, 193
Story Garden (British Library) 22, 42–7, *46–7*
storytelling 22, 23, 38–42, 47
street parties 11, 176, 179
sustainability 15, 23, 53, 71, 97
and housing 114, 115, 116, 120
sustainable neighbourhoods 116, 118–19, 120, 123

Tailoring Academy (Harringay) 70, 94–111, *98–9, 103, 106–7, 108*
and Brexit 101–2
and CEO's role 99, 101, 108
design strategy of *104*
design/manufacturing/retail interlinked at 108–9, *110–111*
education/manufacturing interlinked at *95, 100, 101,* 102–5, *109*
and ethical practices 97, 98, 101
and Fashion Enter 97–101
and Galaxius (performance-related pay system) 101
and micro-factory concept 108, 109
and printing technology 105–8
qualifications offered by 96, 102
and Stitching Academy 102
in Wales 96, 99–101, 105
Taylor, Rachael *21, 25, 28–9, 39, 42*
Thornhill Foundation 71, 74, 80
Thornhill Library (Islington) 71, 72–92, *86–7, 90–91*
children in design process for *82–3, 85*

and children reading *73, 77,* 84
and community 74, 75–6, 80–81, 84, 92
fundraising for 76, 79–80, 81–4, *89*
and government cuts 70, 74, 75
lesson to other schools from 89–92
and Little free Library 76, 78–9
and mission of Thornhill Primary School *73,* 74, 75
and parents' skills 75, 76, 78
and poetry book project 76–8
and PTA 76, 79, 84
resistance to 89
and running project 80, 81–4, *88*
town planning 11, 14–15, 168, 206
Transport for London 15, 179

ULEZ (Ultra Low Emission Zone) scheme 195
urban farms *see* food production
urbanism 15, 62, 160, 173, 184
grass-roots/bottom-up 13, 206
guerrilla 172
temporary 168

Verma, Anurag 70, 114, 115, *115,* 117–18, 119, 120, *120,* 121–3
volunteering 132, 191, 198
and community gardens 23, 25, 27, *30, 32*
and food production 50, 52, *53,* 61
and self-build housing 114, 117, 128
Vyvial, Valerie *35, 44, 45*

Wales 96, 99–101, 105, 191
Walters Way (Lewisham) 114, 115, 119–120, 128
Wandsworth 11, 190
Wandsworth Food Partnership 191, 193
well-being 11, 12, 13, 15, 55, 120, 160
Wood Green *see* Blue House Yard
Woodlands Farm Trust 52–3, 61

young people 159–60, 192, 203
and education/training 22, 25–7, 101, 157
marginalised/hard-to-reach 14, 15, 25, 32, 191, 192, 198